NEH

MW01535241

Robertson's Notes

Bible Books 16 of 66

A Bible Book Commentary

By

John C Robertson

Contents

Abbreviations

AG	Arndt and Gingrich, A Greek-English Lexicon of the NT
AHD	American Heritage Dictionary
ASV	1901 American Standard Version Bible
ESV	English Standard Version
Friberg	Analytical Greek New Testament - Interlinear and Grammatical Analysis
ISBE	International Standard Bible Encyclopedia
KJV	King James Version Bible
LS	Liddell and Scott, A Greek-English Lexicon of the NT
Moulton	The Analytical Greek Lexicon
NM	Nestle and Marshall Interlinear Greek-English NT

FOREWORD

The objective of Robertson's notes is to explain Bible text in a precise and simple format. You will not read opinions, personal convictions, preconceived religious ideas, or a dogma of a particular denominational body. You will find a study that permits the word of God to explain itself. An expositor's best tools are context, cross references, terms of equivalences, and defining the original Greek meaning of words. Any study of God's word must take fearful consideration of the authoritative nature of divine revelation. God is the sovereign creator of earth and time. No man has the right to add or subtract from the mind of God.

Using Robertson's notes affectively means understanding the simple system of references and studies. The reader will encounter abbreviations for references used in parenthesis with their corresponding page number such as (Moulton 340). The reader will also encounter English words with the translated Greek word in parenthesis. Sometimes the author has written this out as follows, "deacon (Greek *diakon*)." Other times the Greek word stands alone as follows (*diakon*). Greek words will always be in italics and their respective definitions given. There are questions at the end of each chapter so that the reader may have a complete Bible study of the text.

There are also parenthetical studies that are referenced at the end of this book titled, "Bible Topics Index." The reader will encounter parenthetical numbers that corresponds to the appropriate Special Study as follows, (30p). When you come across these parenthesis with a number simply look to the back of this book for the study reference. A separate book examines these special studies in detailed fashion.

Lastly, the Bible text used in this study is the 1901 American Standard Version Bible (ASV) unless otherwise noted. The ASV is recognized as a "Formal Equivalence" text as opposed to a "Dynamic Equivalence." The Formal Equivalence method of translating Bible text into another language occurs by taking the original words and moving them over to the target language without too much concern over continuity and fluidity of reading. This is known as a "literal translation" or a "word for word translation" of God's word. The Dynamic Equivalence method of translating the Greek to English language occurs by translating the original language into the target language by means of paraphrasing the meaning. The value of a Formal Equivalence text is that human thought is removed from the meaning of the original words. The words say what they originally said rather than what someone paraphrases them to say. The author has taken the liberty to remove all archaic words such as "thee," "thou," "saith," and so forth seeing that the ASV is in the public domain.

NEHEMIAH

"So we built the wall; and all the wall was joined together unto half the height thereof: for the people had a mind to work"

Nehemiah 4:6

Introduction

We may read the book of Nehemiah and come away with a general appreciation for a man's conviction and spiritual energy to get work accomplished and move on to another story. Yet if we do not pause and contemplate the historical events as a whole we will miss out on encouraging information. Nehemiah is a story of a man who understood the concept of obeying God and performing duties. He was a man who truly cared about God and his people. The modern world we live in lacks people with genuine care. We may find a charity for every known cause and find many individuals who have dedicated their lives to helping the less fortunate in this world. One may conclude that truly there is care in the modern world. Yet when one looks to the grand spiritual picture of life, death, and eternity there seems to be a void of individuals who have genuine care for the eternal souls of men. Jesus said, *"The harvest indeed is plenteous but the laborers are few"* (Matthew 9:37).

1

Many are too busy to care about a neighbor's soul. Today's Christians often found tending only to the affairs of their own lives. We have bills to pay, investments to make, shopping to do, and entertainment to get us through this life. We look for encouragement from heroes on the big screen movies and novels of historical figures of years gone by that were viewed as successful in this world. A look at Nehemiah will not inspire me to achieve great strides in science, mathematics, theater, music, athleticism, and or financial success. The few years of Nehemiah's covered in this book will; however, help me to see that if I try in this life I can make a spiritual difference in the lives of others. Nehemiah was a man who recognized that when the duty of God's laws call we have no recourse but to follow divine instructions. The message of the book is that no matter who seeks to discourage me from doing God's work I must perform my duty (see Nehemiah 4:6 and 10:28-29, 39).

Date of Book

Nehemiah was a Jewish captive and served as the cup bearer to King Artaxerxes during the twentieth year of his reign (444 BC / see notes below at Kings of Persia) (Nehemiah 1:11; 2:1). The Artaxerxes of the days of Nehemiah is the same Artaxerxes as found in the book of Ezra due to Ezra and Nehemiah's joint participation in Jerusalem (see Nehemiah 8:9 and 12:26, 36). The dates add up as well. It took Zerubbabel approximately 44 total years to build the temple (compare Ezra 1:1; 3:8; and 6:15). Ezra spent one year correcting the erroneous marriages of the people (45 total years / i.e., from the first year of Cyrus to the sixth year of Darius) (compare Ezra 7:9 to Ezra 10:9, 17). Twelve years exists between the writing of Ezra and Nehemiah (compare Ezra 7:7-9; 10:9, 17 with Nehemiah 2:2). The date of Nehemiah is thereby 444 BC and encompasses a span of approximately twelve years (compare Nehemiah 2:2 with 13:6).

Consider the kings of Persia

Cyrus (559 [536 over Babylon] – 530 BC) – Allowed Jews to return to Jerusalem, under the leadership of Zerubbabel, to rebuild the temple (Ezra 1:1-2). The Jews efforts were frustrated all the days of Cyrus (Ezra 4:5).

Cambyses (530 – 522 BC) (the Ahasuerus or Xerxes of Ezra 4:6-23) – Killed his brother Smerdis to secure his position as King of Persia. Cambyses received letters from the Samaritans in relation to the construction of the temple. He authorized a decree to cease the work on the temple due to the history of Jewish rebellion in Jerusalem (Ezra 4:19-21).

Gomates (Pseudo-Smerdis) (521 BC) – Laid claims to being the murdered brother of Cambyses and usurped the throne of Cambyses while he was away in Egypt. Gomates was quickly killed by a Persian officer. His rule did not lasts but for a few months.

Darius the Great (521 -486 BC) – During the second year of Darius (i.e., 519 BC) Haggai and Zechariah prophesied unto the Jews in Judah and Jerusalem and encouraged them to return to the work of the temple (Ezra 4:24-5:1). Tattenai (the governor beyond the River / Ezra 5:3) questioned the validity of the work. The governor writes a letter to Darius requesting that a search be made in the Persian archives as to whether or not Cyrus ever gave a decree that the temple should be constructed (cf. Ezra 5:17). Darius found that Cyrus did give such a decree (Ezra 6:3) and so he gave authority to Zerubbabel and the Jews to continue the work (Ezra 6:14). Four years latter, the sixth year of Darius, the temple was completed (Ezra 6:15).

Artaxerxes / Ahasuerus / Xerxes (485 - 465 BC) – Persian king that reigned during the days of Esther and Mordecai (events that transpire between Ezra 6:22 and 7:1).

3

Artaxerxes I Longimanus (464 – 424 BC) – During the year 457 BC (seventh year of Artaxerxes) the King allowed Ezra to return to Jerusalem to inquire of the spiritual well being of the people (Ezra 7:7-9, 14). Within one year Ezra accomplishes spiritual reform in 100 families that had involved themselves in unlawful marriages (compare Ezra 7:9 with 10:9 and 10:17). The book of Ezra ends during the eighth year of the reign of Artaxerxes (i.e., 456 BC). Twelve years latter we are introduced to Nehemiah (i.e., the twentieth year of Artaxerxes {444 BC} / see Nehemiah 2:1). Nehemiah's objective was to construct the wall around Jerusalem and he accomplishes this feat, with the help of God, in 52 days (Nehemiah 6:15). The wall is dedicated to Jehovah God (Nehemiah 12) and Nehemiah returns to the king to serve as cup bearer as he had promised he would (Nehemiah 2:6). Nehemiah had remained in Jerusalem for 12 years (i.e., the thirty second year of Artaxerxes {432 BC} / see Nehemiah 13:6).

Nehemiah the Man

Nehemiah received word that the wall around Jerusalem remained in ruins 57 years after the captives returned to Jerusalem (Nehemiah 1:3) (i.e., 45 years to build the temple and spiritually restore the people plus 12 years between the writing of Ezra and Nehemiah). We are introduced to Nehemiah's convictions when he responds to the news of the ruined walls with weeping, fasting, and prayer (Nehemiah 1:4-11). God had commanded that the walls be constructed (Ezra 6:14; 9:9) and after 57 years they remained in ruins. It is apparent from Ezra 5:3 that God's people had been slowly working upon the wall yet with little progress (Nehemiah 2:16). With the providential help of God Nehemiah completes the wall project in 52 days (see Nehemiah 2:8 and 6:15). It is during this fifty two day period that we find out much about Nehemiah's true Character. Nehemiah was laughed at (Nehemiah 2:19), mocked (Nehemiah 4:1-3), threatened

(Nehemiah 4:11), plotted against (Nehemiah 6:1ff), falsely accused (Nehemiah 6:5-8), and intimidated by the enemies of God (Nehemiah 6:9, 13, 19) yet he remained determined to accomplish God's will of building the wall (Nehemiah 4:14). A sense of duty and obedience to God were a great part of Nehemiah's character (Nehemiah 2:5, 17-18; 4:6; 5:16; 6:3 and 10:29). Nehemiah was a man of great faith (Nehemiah 2:20) and prayer (Nehemiah 1:5-11; 2:4 and 4:4, 9). He was confident in God's providential care (Nehemiah 2:2-4, 8, 18), bold to do what is right (Nehemiah 2:5ff; 4:14), one who hated sin (Nehemiah 4:4-5), and exposed sin whenever it rose its ugly head (Nehemiah 5:6-7). Nehemiah was also deeply concerned about the spiritual (Nehemiah 1:3-4) and physical (Nehemiah 5:10, 14, 17) well being of God's people.

We study through twelve years of Nehemiah's life only to come to a climax in his character at chapter 13 of this book. God's people were guilty of three counts of disobedience. Nehemiah corrects each of their errors and ends each case with the common denominator phrase, "*Remember me, O my God, concerning this... spare me according to the greatness of your lovingkindness*" (Nehemiah 13:14, 22, 31). Nehemiah understood that duties belong to the individual and each will be responsible for their own actions. If each of us as Christians would gain greater understanding of this fact then we may have a greater outlook on life and eternity. I cannot control what others do but I can control what I do. Duties belong to me as an individual. When others are angry at me, laugh, mock, or even threaten me because of my faith I must press forward and perform my God ordained duties. Nehemiah was this kind of a person. One may say that the book of Nehemiah is a handbook for elders and those aspiring to be elders. Others may say Nehemiah is a book that encourages Christians of all genders and races to perform their God given duties no matter the consequences. The message of the book is clear and simple. When God gives a command let us do all within our power to achieve his will and bring glory to his most holy name.

NEHEMIAH CHAPTER 1

Synopsis

Nehemiah's reaction to the people's sin of not building the wall around Jerusalem is very informative. Building the wall was a matter of right and wrong in the eyes of God. Nehemiah knew this and prays fervently to God, as did Ezra, that he and the people may be forgiven. He knew that there was an inseparable connection between God's grace and man's obedience. God's grace and mercy are removed from those who will not meet their responsibility of obedience. God's grace and mercy belong to those who sin, acknowledge the error, and repent. Nehemiah's prayer teaches us elementary principles of the grace and mercy of God. He determines to do something about the Jew's negligence so that God's favor may be restored to the people.

Application

The book of Romans chapter 6 ties an inseparable relationship between grace, forgiveness, law, and obedience. Man may serve many religious laws in this life yet there is but one that offers the forgiveness of sins and that is the "*law of faith*" (Romans 3:27). God's high expectation is that man attain an equivalent righteousness to his very own (see Romans 3:20-21). This is why Jesus commanded that his disciples be just as perfect as God (Matthew 5:48). The Apostle Peter wrote that Christians were to be just as holy as God (1 Peter 1:15-16). He said that we are to attain unto a divine nature just like God (2 Peter 1:4). The Apostle John wrote that Christians are to be

6

just as God in this world we live in (1 John 4:17). Paul explains how attaining the righteousness and holiness of God is possible at Romans 6. When people are baptized they are forgiven, justified, and or made righteous just as God. Baptized people die to sin and purpose not to return to that form of living. When error does occur they may be forgiven through repentance and prayer. Obedience to God's laws is very important and Nehemiah knew this.

Nehemiah 1

News regarding the Walls of Jerusalem and the Affliction of the people reach the ears of Nehemiah (1:1-3)

"**1** *The words of Nehemiah the son of Hacaliah. Now it came to pass in the month Chislev, in the twentieth year, as I was in Shushan the palace,* **2** *that Hanani, one of my brethren, came, he and certain men out of Judah; and I asked them concerning the Jews that had escaped, that were left of the captivity, and concerning Jerusalem*" **(1:1-2).**

The "*twentieth year*" of Artaxerxes would be 444 BC (see also Nehemiah 2:1). Twelve years after Ezra completed the reformation of illegal marriages among God's people we have the events of the book of Nehemiah (see Ezra 7:7). The month Chislev would be the ninth month of the year which corresponds to our December. Zerubbabel came to Jerusalem to rebuild the city's walls and temple during the year 536 BC. Twenty one years later the temple is completed yet the walls of the city remain in ruins (518 BC). There is a 57 year gap between Ezra chapters 6 and 7 (likely the events of Esther took place). If we were to subtract the current date of 444 BC from the initial date that Zerubbabel returned to Jerusalem we get roughly 90 years. It has been ninety years since the captives were permitted to return to Jerusalem and the walls have not yet been constructed.

Nehemiah was in the palace located in Shushan (or Susa). Shushan means "the fortress" or "citadel." Susa was one of three principle or capital cities of the Persian Empire. Nehemiah is identified as a

Jewish "*cup bearer*" to the king of Persia and later he is appointed as governor over Judah (Nehemiah 1:11; 5:14 and 12:26). Hanani was Nehemiah's physical brother in the flesh (see Nehemiah 7:2). Hanani and others had just arrived in Susa from Judah. Nehemiah is anxious to know about the conditions of his brethren in Judah and Jerusalem.

"**3** *And they said unto me, The remnant that are left of the captivity there in the province are in great affliction and reproach: the wall of Jerusalem also is broken down, and the gates thereof are burned with fire*" **(1:3).**

The Jews that had returned with Zerubbabel to build the temple and those that returned with Ezra had repopulated and remodeled the war torn area of Jerusalem and Judah. They had began a half hearted attempt to rebuild the city of Jerusalem's walls yet not much was accomplished (see Ezra 4:12-16). The earlier trouble that the Jews experienced with the Samaritans continues (see Ezra 4:1-4; Nehemiah 2:19 and 4:1ff). The remnant was being afflicted, reproached, and unwilling or able to reconstruct the walls of the city.

Nehemiah's Response to his brother's Bad News (1:4-11)

"**4** *And it came to pass, when I heard these words, that I sat down and wept, and mourned certain days; and I fasted and prayed before the God of heaven*" **(1:4).**

Nehemiah's reaction to the news was threefold. First, he wept because his brethren were being afflicted and because the wall of Jerusalem lay in waste. Secondly, Nehemiah mourned certain days (for days he was in a state of depression due to this news). Thirdly, he fasted (i.e., he went without food for an unspecified time) and prayed to God. Such a reaction reminds us of Ezra's response to hearing that the people of God had sinned by taking foreign women as wives (see Ezra 9:1ff). Sometimes it takes a few "*days*" for people to mourn over a painful situation and then a plan of action comes.

No doubt it saddened Nehemiah that the people were being afflicted yet why would the cup bearer pray to God in relation to sin in the next few verses? It seems apparent that just as it was a commandment to rebuild the temple of Jehovah in Jerusalem it was likewise a commandment to rebuild the walls (see Ezra 6:14). To leave off building the wall would not only cause Jerusalem to be vulnerable to their enemies but be guilty of violating God's will. Ninety years had passed since the remnant of Jews had returned to the city of Jerusalem with the intentions of not only restoring the temple of God but to also reconstruct the walls around the city.

*"**5** and said, I beseech you, O Jehovah, the God of heaven, the great and terrible God, **that keeps covenant and lovingkindness with them that love him and keep his commandments**: 6 let your ear now be attentive, and your eyes open, that you may hear the prayer of your servant, which I pray before you at this time, day and night, for the children of Israel your servants, while I confess the sins of the children of Israel, which we have sinned against you. Yea I and my father's house have sinned"* **(1:5-6).**

God had given Israel the *"covenant"* law of commandments at Mount Sinai and expected the people to obey them (see Deuteronomy 4:12-13 and 5:1-3). The Lord promised to bless the people with protection and eventually a savior to remove all their sins (see Acts 22-26 as Peter quotes from Deuteronomy 9:15-19). The early principles of God's grace and mercy are identified in these early verses. Nehemiah's prayer illustrates a connection between God's loving kindness (grace) and man's obedience. Grace and mercy is given by God to those who do not deserve it yet without efforts of obedience man is without God's favors (see Ezekiel 36:22-23, 26-32). God's laws and grace are illustrated to be inseparably connected by the prophet Isaiah. Isaiah identifies God's everlasting covenant as the *"sure mercies of David"* at Isaiah 54:3. The Apostle Paul identified the *"sure mercies of David"* as the forgiveness of sins at Acts 13:33-39. To receive God's grace, the forgiveness of sins, one must be baptized (please follow the progression of teaching from Ephesians 2:8 to 1:7 to Acts 2:38) (13a).

Nehemiah is deeply concerned about the people of Israel's stand before Jehovah God. The people have not kept God's commandments and were in sin. God's lovingkindness (his grace) is for those who "*love him and keep his commandments*." Jesus said the same thing at John 14:15. The Lord said, "*If you love me you will keep my commandments*." To restore the people to the favor and grace of God they needed forgiveness. Nehemiah proves himself to be a meek man by humbling himself before God and confessing his sins and the sins of the people.

"**7** *We have dealt very corruptly against you, and have not kept the commandments, nor the statutes, nor the ordinances, which you commanded your servant Moses.* **8** *Remember, I beseech you, the word that you commanded your servant Moses, saying,* **If** *you trespass, I will scatter you abroad among the peoples:* **9** *but* **if** *you* **return unto me, and keep my commandments and do them**, *though your outcasts were in the uttermost part of the heavens, yet will I gather them from thence, and will bring them unto the place that I have chosen, to cause my name to dwell there*" **(1:7-9).**

Moses laid down the laws of God to the people. The Lord had high expectations of the people's perfect obedience (see Deuteronomy 27:26 and Galatians 3:10). There were grave consequences for those who rebelled against God's laws. Moses writes, "33 *and you will I scatter among the nations, and I will draw out the sword after you: and your land shall be a desolation, and your cities shall be a waste*" (Leviticus 26:33). Though God would scatter, slash with the sword, and lay waste their cities he would not forget them. Those who would see the error of their way and repent would be restored to the Lord's favor (see Deuteronomy 30:1-5). Nehemiah's objective of his prayer is to regain the favor of God. The man of God knows that the only way to do this is with true repentance; i.e., "*return unto me*." Notice the equivalence between "*return*" and "*keep and do my commandments.*" When someone repents of wrongdoing they stop doing the wrong.

There are many similar "*if*" statements in the New Testament that reveal the connection between God's grace and man's obedience (see Colossians 1:22-23 and 1 Corinthians 15:1-2). God's grace continues to work the same way today. The Lord demands that those who sin acknowledge their error and repent (see Luke 13:5 and Acts 17:30). Baptism is the initial acts of obedience that brings one in contact with God's grace or the forgiveness of sins (see Acts 2:38; 22:16; Ephesians 1:7; 2:8; and 1 Peter 3:21). The consequence of not having God's grace and favor is death, scattering, desolation, and cities being laid waste (Romans 2:5ff). Surely all can see these early principles of how God's grace works (13b).

"**10** *Now these are your servants and your people, whom you have redeemed by your great power, and by your strong hand.* **11** *O Lord, I beseech you, let now your ear be attentive to the prayer of your servant, and to the prayer of your servants, who delight to fear your name; and prosper, I pray, your servant this day, and grant him mercy in the sight of this man. Now I was cupbearer to the king*" **(1:10-11).**

Nehemiah identifies the remnant, that returned to Judah from Babylon, as those the Lord has redeemed by his "*great power.*" God had promised that a remnant would return before the seventy years of captivity had even begun (Jeremiah 29:8-10). The omniscience and power of God are depicted in the fact that he speaks the end from the beginning (see Isaiah 46:9-10). Nehemiah reminds the Lord that Israel was his people and he had loved them enough to bring them out of Babylonian captivity to rebuild the city, its walls, and temple.

Nehemiah is determined to resolve the people's sinful delinquency of not building the city's walls. He plans to go before king Artaxerxes to make request regarding the walls of Jerusalem. Nehemiah's profession of "*cupbearer*" afforded him an opportunity to go before the king. The Persian "*cupbearer*" is identified as "Hebrew being 'one giving drink.' An officer of high rank at ancient oriental courts, whose duty it was to serve the wine at the king's table. On account of the constant fear of plots and intrigues, a person must be regarded as thoroughly trustworthy to hold this position. He must guard against poison in the king's cup, and was sometimes required to swallow some of the wine before serving it. His confidential relations with the king often endeared him to his sovereign and also gave him a position of great influence" (ISBE, volume 1, page 837). Nehemiah was no stranger to the king of Persia.

Questions over Nehemiah Chapter 1

1. Who was Nehemiah?

2. What as Nehemiah's reaction to hearing that the walls and gates of Jerusalem were broken down?

3. Why did Nehemiah react this way?

4. What sins had the people of Israel committed against God?

5. **True or False:** There is no connection between Gods' grace and man's responsibility to follow God's commandments.

NEHEMIAH CHAPTER 2

Synopsis

God had promised great blessings, through Isaiah, to the remnant in Babylonian captivity. Zerubbabel led thousands of people back to Jerusalem, by the providential care of God, to rebuild the temple. Ezra led many back to Jerusalem to restore spiritual morality. Ezra was also providentially cared for by God. Now we find Nehemiah returning the Jerusalem with the same favor of God.

Nehemiah chapter two reveals a deep seated hatred that the enemies of God had for the Jews. The Samaritans were not permitted to help rebuild the temple of God and neither are they welcome to have any say so in the rebuilding of the wall around Jerusalem (Nehemiah 2:19-20). The stage will be set for a show down between the haters of God and the Lord's people. The walls around Jerusalem would go up and there was nothing the ungodly could do to stop it.

Application

Today, God continues to providentially bless his people with opportunities to preach and teach the word of God. Many; however, are very annoyed with the message of the cross. The Lord's message is that man change his own personal opinions regarding spiritual matters and get back to the authority of God.

Another application to note at Nehemiah chapter two is the exclusive nature of the Lord's church today. Those who do not hold to the teachings of Jesus Christ are not a part of the Christian community of believers (see 2 John 9-11). Nehemiah was very careful to keep God's people sanctified from those of the world who lay claims to loving and obeying God yet they really do not (see also 2 Corinthians 6:14-7:1). Jesus said that the real test of one's love for the Lord is whether or not that person obeys God's commandments (see John 14:15). Jesus also prayed that all who truly love God's commandments would remain one in purpose (John 17:14-23). The only way for God's church to work is through people of like precious faith working toward the same ends (Ephesians 4:16).

Nehemiah 2

Artaxerxes Grants Nehemiah's Request (2:1-8)

"**1** *And it came to pass in the month Nisan, in the twentieth year of Artaxerxes the king, when wine was before him, that I took up the wine, and gave it unto the king. Now I had not been beforetime sad in his presence*" **(2:1).**

The month Nisan corresponds to our March and is three months after Nehemiah had received news regarding the walls of Jerusalem (see Nehemiah 1:1).

One who personally serves the king of the great Persian Empire would not want to appear before the king in a state of sadness. Such a king had the affairs of the Empire, and at times his own life, to worry about much less the individual troubles of a servant. To be sad before the king may prove detrimental to the servant. Nehemiah had previously been of a joyful spirit when around the king; however, there were things now that deeply bothered him.

"**2** *And the king said unto me, Why is your countenance sad, seeing you are not sick? This is nothing else but sorrow of heart. Then I was very sore afraid.* **3** *And I said unto the king, Let the king live for ever:*

why should not my countenance be sad, when the city, the place of my father's sepulchers, lies waste, and the gates thereof are consumed with fire? **4** *Then the king said unto me, For what do you make request? So I prayed to the God of heaven"* **(2:2-4).**

The fact that the king of Persia was personally asking Nehemiah questions indicates the high level of importance and trust a cupbearer held. Not many of us today could say that we have conversations with the president of the United States.

The king took notice of Nehemiah's sad state. Nehemiah's sadness was obviously not due to any sickness. The king concludes that the cupbearer's sadness must be due to "*sorrow of heart.*" The prayer of Nehemiah's at chapter 1:6-11 is already being answered. Nehemiah has the attention of the king albeit it is a dangerous situation and so he is fearful. Nehemiah must have concluded that if the walls of Jerusalem were to be built the people needed to be moved to do so. If he did not decide to be the motivator then who would it be? The king's cupbearer takes advantage of his close association with the king and puts himself in a position where such a request might be made. Nehemiah was depending upon the providence of God to see to it that his request might be given an approval. Nehemiah was confident that God would providentially provide Israel with a way to fulfill the command to build a wall around Jerusalem.

Note the great faith in Nehemiah as he said a quick prayer before answering the king of Persia. We may learn a valuable lesson here regarding the state of one's faith. When dealing with God's commandments and the souls of men we ought to take the time to pray to God that conditions might be made favorable so that the saints and lost souls may repent and do those things necessary for salvation. The spiritual and physical condition of God's people was in jeopardy and so Nehemiah prayed. The prayer may have been a quick, "Lord, I pray that you grant me favor this day in the hearing of the king that your walls may be constructed."

*"**5** And I said unto the king, if it please the king, and if your servant has found favor in your sight, that you would send me unto Judah, unto the city of my fathers' sepulchers, that I may build it"* **(2:5).**

Nehemiah addresses the king of Persia with respect for the position he held and made a request to return to Jerusalem and build the city. Earlier he said, *"Let the king live forever"* (Nehemiah 2:3). If Nehemiah could go to Jerusalem, by the authority of Artaxerxes, surely the antagonistic enemies would not be allowed to bother the Jews. Note that Nehemiah's request was that he alone be the man in charge of such an endeavor. Nehemiah, like so many faithful men before him, was God's man of the hour. Nehemiah likely knew of Artaxerxes' awareness and fear of Jehovah God as was twelve years previously displayed in the king's words to Ezra (see Ezra 7:23).

*"**6** And the king said unto me (the queen also sitting by him), For how long shall your journey be? And when will you return? So it pleased the king to send me; and I set him a time. **7** Moreover I said unto the king, if it please the king, let letters be given me to the governors beyond the River, that they may let me pass through till I come unto Judah; **8** and a letter unto Asaph the keeper of the king's forest, that he may give me timber to make beams for the gates of the castle which appertains to the house, and for the wall of the city, and for the house that I shall enter into. And the king granted me, according to the good hand of my God upon me"* **(2:6-8).**

Artaxerxes was no stranger to the proceedings at Jerusalem. The king had earlier written a decree on behalf of Ezra that the priestly scribe would go to Jerusalem and *"**14** inquire concerning Judah and Jerusalem, according to the law of your God which is in your hand..."* (Ezra 7:14). Ezra recognized such actions on the part of the king of Persia to be the providence of God (Ezra 7:27). Once again the king of Persia grants permission for a multitude of Jews to leave the area of Mesopotamia and Persia that they may improve the conditions in Judah. Nehemiah, as did Ezra before him, recognized these grants to be in accordance with the providence of God (see Nehemiah 2:8 compared to Ezra 7:27) (3b).

The king grants all of Nehemiah's requests. First, Nehemiah asks to be sent to Jerusalem of Judah to rebuild the city (Nehemiah 2:5). Secondly, Nehemiah asks the king to provide letters that may be given to the governors beyond the Euphrates River that they may know that permission has been granted for such a journey (Nehemiah 2:7). Thirdly, Nehemiah asks the king for letters to give to Asaph (the keeper of the king's forest - an OT timber manager) so that materials may be supplied to build gates for the temple of Jehovah, the wall around the city of Jerusalem, and for a house that he shall dwell in.

Nehemiah travels to Jerusalem and Assesses the Job at Hand (2:9-16)

"*9 Then I came to the governors beyond the River, and gave them the king's letters. Now the king had sent with me captains of the army and horsemen. 10 And when Sanballat the Horonite, and Tobiah the servant, the Ammonite, heard of it, it grieved them exceedingly, for that there was come a man to seek the welfare of the children of Israel*" **(2:9-10).**

Not much is said of the journey to Jerusalem other than the fact that as Nehemiah reached the governors west of the Euphrates River he delivered the letters from Artaxerxes to them for safe passage. Secondly, we are told that Nehemiah, unlike Ezra (Ezra 8:22), had a military escort.

Sanballat and Tobiah are "*exceedingly grieved*" that someone has come to "*seek the welfare of the children of Israel.*" "Sanballat's name in the Hebrews language literally means 'may sin give him life.' A Horonite who led the Samaritan opposition to the rebuilding of Jerusalem walls in the days of Nehemiah (Nehemiah 2:10, 19; 4:1ff; 6:1ff) and governor of Syria in the Aramaic papyri from Elephantine... Since Sanballat is named together with Tobiah the Ammonite and

Geshem the Arab (Nehemiah 2:19 and 4:7), it is quite possible that he was a Moabite" (ISBE volume 4, page 320).

Tobiah was "An ally of Sanballat the Horonite and Geshem the Arab, chief oppoints of Nehemiah's efforts to rebuild the walls of the postexilic Jerusalem... The reference here to Ammon signifies his jurisdiction over Ammonite territory, not his ancestry. It is possible that Tobiah was a descendant of Jews who had fled to Ammon after the sack of Jerusalem (Jeremiah 41:15)... By marriage both Tobiah and his son were related to influential segments of Jewish nobility, many bound to him by oath, and these spoke well of him to Nehemiah (6:17-19). This may explain why Tobiah was allowed to occupy a chamber in the temple precincts during Nehemiah's absence from Jerusalem (13:4-9)... Nehemiah incurred the hostility of Tobiah, Sanballat, and Geshem, because by restoring Judah to a place of equal standing with their provinces he was threatening their status and economic power in the region" (ISBE volume 4, page 865).

"**11** *So I came to Jerusalem, and was there three days.* **12** *And I arose in the night, I and some few men with me; neither told I any man what my God put into my heart to do for Jerusalem; neither was there any beast with me, save the beast that I rode upon*" **(2:11-12).**

Nehemiah, like Ezra, takes a three day rest from the journey (Ezra 8:32). Having told no one of his resolution to rebuild the city walls, he takes an opportunity to access the condition of the walls by night. Nehemiah wanted to know the magnitude of his project in which he was to soon reveal to the people.

Nehemiah said that his work in Jerusalem was due to God putting it into his heart to do. Nehemiah was a man of great faith. He knew God's will regarding the city of Jerusalem. Nehemiah volunteered for the job because he knew the will of God regarding building the city and its walls. Nehemiah was like Isaiah (see Isaiah 6:8) and Ezra (Ezra 7:6, 10) in that he saw a spiritual duty that needed a worker and he did it. The church today needs spiritually minded men and women who see the necessity to teach the gospel and just do it (Romans 1:16).

"**13** *And I went out by night by the valley gate, even toward the jackal's well, and to the dung gate, and viewed the walls of Jerusalem, which were broken down and the gates thereof were consumed with fire.* **14** *Then I went on to the fountain gate and to the king's pool: but there was no place for the beast that was under me to pass.* **15** *Then went I up in the night by the brook, and viewed the wall; and I turned back, and entered by the valley gate, and so returned.* **16** *And the rulers knew not whither I went, or what I did; neither had I as yet told it to the Jews, nor to the priests, nor to the nobles, nor to the rulers, nor to the rest that did the work*" **(2:13-16).**

Nehemiah travels from the "*valley gate*" to the "*dung gate*" on to the "*fountain gate and to the king's pool.*" The city of David sat upon the top of Mount Zion and was similar in shape to the state of Florida. The city was surrounded by a wall that had eight gates. The three gates mentioned above are found on the south side of the city. Nehemiah tours the south side of the city, takes some notes, and returns to his sleeping quarters with none of the rulers of the city knowing what he had done.

Why did Nehemiah do this in the night? Why didn't he tell any of the Jews, priests, nobles, rulers, or any who did the work on the wall? The reason is very clear. The work of the city's walls was ongoing, though at an unsatisfactory pace, even as Nehemiah has arrived. The Lord's original objective for the returning remnant was to rebuild the temple, city, and its walls (see Ezra 9:9). Zerubbabel had returned to Jerusalem during the year 536 BC by permission of Cyrus to begin the work. After 21 years the temple is finally finished (compare Ezra 1:1; 3:8; and 6:15) (i.e., the year 515 BC). Ezra comes on the scene 57 years latter (i.e., during the reign of Artaxerxes king of Persia (Ezra 7:1) (458 BC). One year latter Ezra completes his work of religious reforms (compare Ezra 7:9 with Ezra 10:17) (457 BC). Approximately 12 years latter the walls are still not built as the Word of God introduces Nehemiah (Nehemiah 1:1ff) (445 BC). A total of 91 years have passed without the wall around Jerusalem being completed.

The work of restoring the wall was in progress according to Nehemiah 2:16. The people of God were obviously piddling around with the building process. A plausible reason for the slow progress is the clear antagonism on the part of the Samaritans. They had been successful in completely halting the building of the temple for 15 years during the days of Zerubbabel (Ezra 4:24) and are now succeeding in at least slowing the work on the wall. Another reason would be that there was very little significance placed on the wall project by the people. It may have been that only a handful of convicted people were working on the project. Nehemiah comes into an area where the work has not been completed for over 91 years. He knows that there are rulers, priests, and nobles that were in place yet they had not succeeded in completing God's objective for the walls. Rather than accuse them of sin and usurp their authority he handles the situation as wisely as possible. Esther too had to take a delicate situation and deal wisely (see Esther 4:16).

Nehemiah would have the same work as Haggai and Zechariah in that he must motivate the people to do that which they know needs to be accomplished. To this point, 91 years after the fact, the work was not at a satisfactory pace.

Nehemiah Reveals his plan to Build the Walls of Jerusalem (2:17-20)

"**17** *Then said I unto them, You see **the evil case that we are in**, how Jerusalem lies waste, and the gates thereof are burned with fire: come, and let us build up the wall of Jerusalem, **that we be no more a reproach**.* **18** *And I told them of the hand of my God which was good upon me, as also of the king's words that he had spoken unto me. And they said, Let us rise up and build. So they strengthened their hands for the good work*" **(2:17-18).**

Nehemiah was now ready to reveal his purpose for coming to Jerusalem to the Jews, priests, rulers, and nobles of Jerusalem. He has assessed the task and is now ready to motivate the people to do the work of building the wall. The English Standard Version Bible reads as follows for Nehemiah 2:17, "*Then I said to them, You see the trouble we are in, how Jerusalem lies in ruins with its gates burned. Come, let us build the wall of Jerusalem, that we may no longer suffer derision.*" Nehemiah gives the rulers of Jerusalem four reasons to get busy building the walls of Jerusalem. First, Nehemiah tells the rulers that they are in an "*evil case*" or "trouble." God had commanded that the walls be built and they were not 91 years later (see Ezra 6:14 and 9:9). Secondly, if they would build the walls they would no longer be a reproach or suffer derision (disrespect and mockery). The word "*reproach*" means, "to blame for something, to bring shame upon, or something that causes rebuke or blame" (AHD 1049). The people's lack of motivation and respect for God's laws was the blame for their lack of work. The Samaritans watched the Jews and thought very little of them. The Jews inability to complete the walls around the city was a sign of weakness and incompetence. Thirdly, Nehemiah tells the rulers that God would be with them and he knows this because all the material to build has been supplied. Lastly, they were to build because the Persians have issued a building permit by decree of Artaxerxes to build.

No doubt such news would have been refreshing to the Jews. God is with them and has put into the hearts of the Persians to provide all materials needed to accomplish the tasks. The people respond by saying, "*Let us rise up and build.*"

"**19** *But when Sanballat the Horonite, and Tobiah the servant, the Ammonite, and Geshem the Arabian, heard it, they laughed us to scorn, and despised us, and said, What is this thing that you do? Will you rebel against the king?*" **(2:19).**

Sanballat, Tobiah, and Geshem laugh at Nehemiah's proposal to build the wall. The very thought of making improvements to Jerusalem caused the Samaritans to "*despise*" the Jews. They were jealous and filled with hatred against Jerusalem and what the city represented (see Ezra 4:1-4).

The Samaritans bring an old accusation against the Jews by claiming that they only want to rebuild the city and walls so that they may rebel against Persia (Ezra 4:15-16).

"**20** *Then answered I them, and said unto them, the God of heaven, he will prosper us; therefore we his servants will arise and build: but you have no portion, nor right, nor memorial, in Jerusalem*" **(2:20).**

Nehemiah's proposal to build the wall of Jerusalem and fulfill the commandment of God brings immediate friction between the Jews and the surrounding peoples. Nehemiah's response to the discouraging mockery is very similar to Zerubbabel's when the Samaritans wanted to help build the temple (see Ezra 4:2-4). The book of Ezra refers to the Samaritans as "*the adversaries of Judah and Benjamin*" due to their pluralist approach to the Almighty God (see Ezra 4:1). The Samaritans made a request to Zerubbabel that they be granted the opportunity to help build Jehovah's temple. Their qualifications are sited as, "*for we seek your God as you do; and we sacrifice unto him...*" A reading of 2 Kings 17:27-41 yields a greater understanding as to why this statement, regarding seeking and sacrificing to God, is not the absolute truth. At 2 Kings 17:41 we read, "*41 So these nations feared Jehovah, and served their graven images; their children likewise and their children's children, as did their fathers, so do they unto this day.*" The Samaritans were not only idolaters but they refused to keep the commandments of God (see 2 Kings 17:34). Nehemiah boldly tells the Samaritans, once again, that they have "*no portion, nor right, nor memorial in Jerusalem.*" God's people obeyed the voice of the Lord and served him alone (12cc).

It would have been easy for the Jews to continue in their state of apathy and peace. Nehemiah's proposal meant friction, discomfort, and hostility directed at them. A universal principle is established regarding suffering for doing God's commands is given at 2 Timothy 2:12. The Apostle Paul writes, "*All those who live Godly in Christ Jesus will suffer persecution.*" The Christian today may seek peace at the expense of keeping God's commandments; however, it is a short lived peace in relation to eternity (20p). God's people have a command to expose (Ephesians 5:11) and be separate from sinners and their sin (2 Corinthians 6:14 – 7:1).

Questions over Nehemiah Chapter 2

1. What did king Artaxerxes notice about Nehemiah as he served him wine?

2. What did Nehemiah request of the king?

3. Why did Artaxerxes give Nehemiah everything that he asked for?

4. Who was angry because someone had come from Babylon to seek the welfare of the people?

5. What did Nehemiah secretly do at night when he came to Jerusalem?

6. Who made fun of Nehemiah and the people of Jerusalem for getting to work on the city's walls?

NEHEMIAH CHAPTER 3

Synopsis

The following chapter gives a bird's eye view of the work that transpired on the wall around Jerusalem. We are impressed with the amount of workers and the area that is covered. Working from east, counterclockwise, we find men and women working on every part of the wall around Jerusalem. The people of God did not take a section at a time and work on it but rather attacked the wall as a whole.

Nehemiah uses gates, pools, houses, and towers as land marks to designate where people were working. As we travel around the city examining each section of the wall with its towers, pools and gates we get a better view of early life in Jerusalem. The gates (Hebrew *shaar* meaning 'opening' and Greek *pule* meaning to turn) were generally an arched entrance with deep recesses and seats on either side, was a place of meeting in the ancient towns of the East, where the inhabitants assembled either for social intercourse or to transact public business (New Unger's Bible Dictionary page 458). Nehemiah mentions ten gates around Jerusalem at chapter 3 and then reveals two more at chapter 12. Jerusalem had a total of twelve gates around the city that had various functions. Consider some events in the history of God's people that involved the gates of cities.

Shechem loved Dinah, the daughter of Jacob, yet he was a Hivite (Genesis 34:1-3). Shechem and his father Hamor meet with "*the men of the city at the gate*" and determine to circumcise all Hivites so that he and Dinah may be married (Genesis 34:18-20). We find elders of the people passing judgments and making decisions for the affairs of the city at the gate (Deuteronomy 21:19 and Amos 5:12). Boaz is found conducting business at the city gate with the elders regarding Ruth (Ruth 4:1, 11). Absalom tried to usurp his father David's authority at the gate of the city by giving judgment over matters that belonged to his father (2 Samuel 15:2). Jeremiah's fait was contemplated by men gathered at the gate (Jeremiah 26). The prophet Jeremiah is found lamenting over the elders not gathering at the gates to make decisions during his day (Lamentations 5:14). The gate of a city also served as a popular market place where people bought and sold grain (2 Kings 7:1 and Nehemiah 13:19-21). No gate around the city of Jerusalem was a serious blow to the people's way of life. Without the gates they lacked places to meet and discuss the affairs of men and the city. Without the gates they lacked central market places.

Nehemiah 3

Construction begins on the wall of Jerusalem (3 all):

"**1** *Then Eliashib the high priest rose up with his brethren the priests, and they built the* **sheep gate**; *they sanctified it, and set up the doors of it; even unto the tower of Hammeah they sanctified it, unto the tower of Hananel.* **2** *And next unto him built the men of Jericho. And next to them built Zaccur the son of Imri*" **(3:1-2).**

The high priest Eliashib was "A descendant of David (1 Chronicles 3:24). Head of the eleventh course of priests (1 Chronicles 24:12). The high priest in the time of Nehemiah . He, with his brethren the priests, helped in the rebuilding of the wall. But later he was connected with Tobiah the Ammonite and allowed that enemy of Nehemiah the use of a large chamber in the temple; one of his grandsons, a son of Jehoiada, married a daughter of Sanballat the Horonite and was for this reason expelled from the community by Nehemiah" (ISBE volume 2, page 62-63).

The "*sheep gate*" was the gate in the wall North or Northeast of Jerusalem. Sheep for sacrificial offering were probably led to the temple through this gate" (ISBE volume 4, page 465). Nehemiah describes the construction process of the wall starting at the Sheep Gate and going geographically counterclockwise. There are twelve Gates that surrounded the city of Jerusalem mentioned by Nehemiah in chapters 3 and 12.

"**3** *And the fish gate did the sons of Hassenaah build; they laid the beams thereof, and set up the doors thereof, the bolts thereof, and the bars thereof.* **4** *And next unto them repaired Meremoth the son of Uriah, the son of Hakkoz. And next unto them repaired Meshullam the son of Berechiah, the son of Meshezabel. And next unto them repaired Zadok the son of Baana.* **5** *And next unto them the Tekoites repaired; but their nobles put not their necks to the work of their lord*" **(3:3-5).**

The **fish gate** was repaired by the sons of Hassenaah. "This gate is generally located in the north wall... an unlikely place to sell or deliver fish, if the north wall only extended the width of the temple! Because it is located between Gihon and Ophel in the description of Manaseh's wall, one hesitates to locate it in the north wall, but the most logical place would be between the Ephriam Gate and the temple mount, probably in the Central Valley area of the north wall of Mishneh" (2 Chronicles 33:14 and Zephaniah 1:10)" (ISBE volume 2 page 1015). "It probably took its name from the fact of fish being brought through it on the way to the city, or from the fish market being located near it" (New Unger's Bible Dictionary page 430).

Meremoth, Meshullam, Zadok, and the Tekoites appear to be repairing the wall **between** the **fish gate** and **the old gate** (see next verses).

"**6** *And the old gate repaired Joiada the son of Paseah and Meshullam the son of Besodeiah; they laid the beams thereof, and set up the doors thereof, and the bolts thereof, and the bars thereof.* **7** *And next* unto them repaired Melatiah the Gibeonite, and Jadon the Meronothite, the men of Gibeon, and of Mizpah, that appertained to the throne of the governor beyond the River. **8** Next unto him repaired Uzziel the son of Harhaiah, goldsmiths. And next unto him repaired Hananiah one of the perfumers, and they fortified Jerusalem even unto the **broad wall**. **9** And next unto them repaired Rephaiah the son of Hur, the ruler of half the district of Jerusalem. **10** And next unto them repaired Jedaiah the son of Harumaph, over against his house. And next unto him repaired Hattush the son of Hashabneiah. **11** Malchijah the son of Harim, and Hasshub the son of Pahath-moab, repaired another portion, and the **tower of the furnaces**. **12** And next unto him repaired Shallum the son of Hallohesh, the ruler of half the district of Jerusalem, he and his daughters" **(3:6-12).**

The **old gate** was repaired by Joiada. The "*old gate*" (Hebrew *mishneh*) "if formerly a wall extended westward from the Central Valley to the ridge above Hinnom to which a later wall was added that embraced the more northerly part of the Central Valley this may have been a gate opening between these two parts of the city" (ISBE volume 2, page 1020).

Between the old gate and the **valley gate** many repaired the wall to the "*broad wall*" and the "*tower of the furnaces.*" The "*broad wall*" was "a stretch of Jerusalem's wall between the Tower of Furnaces and the Gate of Ephraim" (ISBE volume 1, page 548). The "*tower of the furnaces*" was in the northwestern part of the city, probably near the Corner Gate and was possibly one of the towers built by Uzziah (2 Chronicles 26:9)" (ISBE volume 2 page 1020). The name suggest that baker's ovens were located in this vicinity (ISBE volume 3, page 622).

"**13** The **valley gate** repaired Hanun, and the inhabitants of Zanoah; they built it, and set up the doors thereof, the bolts thereof, and the bars thereof, and a thousand cubits of the wall unto the **dung gate**" **(3:13).**

Hanun and the inhabitants of Zanoah repaired the **valley gate**. The "*valley gate*" was located on the west wall of the city of Jerusalem and just west of the Dung gate. The "*dung gate*" was known as the "gate of the ash heap, refuse pile, dung hill. This gate would obviously be on the side of the city where it would be least offensive. This certainly was in the Valley of Hinnom at some distance from the king's garden. It is probably to be identified with Jeremiah's Potsherd Gate" (ISBE volume 2, page 1018).

"**14** *And the dung gate repaired Malchijah the son of Rechab, the ruler of the district of Beth-haccherem; he built it, and set up the doors thereof, the bolts thereof, and the bars thereof*" **(3:14)**.

Malchijah was given the duty of repairing all that pertained to the dung gate.

"**15** *And the **fountain gate** repaired Shallun the son of Colhozeh, the ruler of the district of Mizpah; he built it, and covered it, and set up the doors thereof, the bolts thereof, and the bars thereof, and the **wall of the pool of Shelah** by the king's garden, even unto the stairs that go down from **the city of David**"* **(3:15)**.

Shallun repaired both the fountain gate and the wall of the pool of Shelah. The "*fountain gate*" is "probably the one at the lower end of David's City that led to En-rogel, for it was near 'the stairs that go down from the city of David', and it is distinguished from the Water ate on the east" (ISBE volume 2, page 1018). "*The pool of Shelah*" a water reservoir that pooled water from Gihon (the main spring east of the city (Isaiah 7:3). Two older aqueducts were located in the Kidron Valley, antedating Hezekiah's tunnel. To the later of these Isaiah may have been referring when he spoke of 'the waters of Shiloah' (Isaiah 8:6), which may have led to the Pool of Shelah, since the words are derived from the same root" (ISBE volume 2, page 1018).

"**16** *After him repaired Nehemiah the son of Azbuk, the ruler of half the district of Beth-zur, unto the place over against **the sepulchers of**

David, *and unto the pool that was made, and unto the house of the mighty men.* **17** *After him repaired the Levites, Rehum the son of Bani. Next unto him repaired Hashabiah, the ruler of half the district of Keilah, for his district.* **18** *After him repaired their brethren, Bavvai the son of Henadad, the ruler of half the district of Keilah"* **(3:16-18).**

The *"sepulchers of David"* and *"house of mighty men"* was an area where the great kings and warriors of Israel were in tombs within the City of David (see also Ezekiel 43:7-9).

*"***19** *And next to him repaired Ezer the son of Jeshua, the ruler of Mizpah, another portion, over against the* **ascent to the armory** *at the turning of the wall.* **20** *After him Baruch the son of Zabbai earnestly repaired another portion, from the turning of the wall unto the door of the* **house of Eliashib the high priest**. **21** *After him repaired Meremoth the son of Uriah the son of Hakkoz another portion, from the door of the house of Eliashib even to the end of the house of Eliashib.* **22** *And after him repaired the priests, the men of the Plain.* **23** *After them repaired Benjamin and Hasshub over against their house. After them repaired Azariah the son of Maaseiah the son of Ananiah beside his own house.* **24** *After him repaired Binnui the son of Henadad another portion, from the house of Azariah unto the turning of the wall, and unto the corner.* **25** *Palal the son of Uzai repaired over against the turning [of the wall], and* **the tower** *that stands out from the upper house of the king, which is by* **the court of the guard**. *After him Pedaiah the son of Parosh repaired"* **(3:15-25).**

The *"armory"* is "a storehouse for weapons, such as that of Hezekiah (2 Kings 20:13). In Nehemiah 3:19 the test is uncertain (as the temple's treasury or actual storage of weapons)" (ISBE volume 1, page 295). Next to Ezer was Baruch who repaired the part of the wall from the armory to the *"door of the house of Eliashib the high priest."* Many others are mentioned as having repaired portions of the wall of Jerusalem reaching from the house of the high priest to the tower near the king's house to the court of the guard.

"**26** *(Now the Nethinim dwelt in Ophel, unto the place over against the* **water gate** *toward the east, and the tower that stands out).* **27** *After him the Tekoites repaired another portion, over against the* **great tower** *that stands out, and unto the* **wall of Ophel**" **(3:26-27).**

The "*water gate*" was near the "*great tower*" and "*wall of Ophel.*" All of these locations are difficult to know much about because there is not much revealed. The significance for our study is that there were many people involved in working on the wall of Jerusalem as a whole.

"**28** *Above the* **horse gate** *repaired the priests, every one over against his own house.* **29** *After them repaired Zadok the son of Immer over against his own house. And after him repaired Shemaiah the son of Shecaniah, the keeper of the* **east gate.** **30** *After him repaired Hananiah the son of Shelemiah, and Hanun the sixth son of Zalaph, another portion. After him repaired Meshullam the son of Berechiah over against his chamber.* **31** *After him repaired Malchijah one of the goldsmiths unto the house of the Nethinim, and of the merchants, over against the* **gate of Hammiphkad,** *and to the ascent of the corner.* **32** *And between the ascent of the corner and the* **sheep gate** *repaired the goldsmiths and the merchants*" **(3:26-32).**

The "*horse gate*" is "a gate in the old wall of Jerusalem at the east end of the bridge leading from Zion to the Temple perhaps so called because the horses which the kings of Judah had given to the sun were led through it for idolatrous worship (see 2 Kings 23:11)" (ISBE volume 1, page 295).

There are twelve gates in all mentioned by Nehemiah. We have to move to chapter 12 to find the gate of Ephraim and the guard gate (see Nehemiah 12:39).

Questions over Nehemiah Chapter 3

1. The people of Judah began working on the wall around Jerusalem

a. A section at a time (When they finished one section they moved to the next).

b. By dividing the city into two parts.

c. By people working on every section of the city's walls all together.

2. Give details of the sections of the wall and its significance.

3. How many gates did Nehemiah mention?

NEHEMIAH CHAPTER 4

Synopsis

Nehemiah and his fellow Jews get off to a great start on the wall. They complete half of it before intense persecution and discouragement settles in. The enemies of God's people formulate a plan to stop the progress of the faithful Jews yet God puts them in confusion. Nehemiah delivers another motivational speech and the people, once again, are back to work. The threat of invasion never ended though God had confused their plans. Nehemiah and the people work on the wall in shifts while others stand watch for enemies with weapons in their hands. Though dangers abounded the people continued to press forward in their God ordained work.

Application

When people obey the gospel and become a Christian they are often very excited and ready to work. The first sign of discouragement or persecution; however, puts a damper on their zeal. Jesus revealed the true picture of Christian people's lives in the parable of the sower (Matthew 13). Too often good and Godly people permit persecution, tribulation, and or worldliness to stand in their way of spiritual success. The lesson we learn from Nehemiah chapter 4 is that once the Christian's individual work is identified they are to go about that work no matter the degree of tribulation, persecution, or worldliness that occurs all around them. Spiritual pessimism is very contagious and if the saints are not careful they may find themselves caught up in the murmuring of the dissatisfied. Let us learn to love God (Matthew 22:37), be content with our lives (1 Timothy 6:8), and walk by the truth (Ephesians 4:1-4) so that our heavenly reward may be realized (Revelation 2:10).

Nehemiah 4

The Enemies of Jerusalem band together to halt the Progress of Building the Wall and Nehemiah Prays (4:16)

"**1** *But it came to pass that, when Sanballat heard that we were building the wall, he was wroth, and took great indignation, and mocked the Jews*" **(4:1).**

We have already been introduced to Sanballat and Tobiah at Nehemiah 2:19. Sanballat heard of Nehemiah's proposal to build the walls of Jerusalem and responded by "*laughing the Jews to scorn and despising them*" (Nehemiah 2:19). This man's scorn moves to anger and great indignation once the Jews began the work and so he mocks them. When all else fails to detour a good work the fool resorts to mocking and derision.

Sanballat's connection with the Samaritans is depicted in his hateful comments regarding the Jews. Both Sanballat and the Samaritans had a passionate hatred for the Jews. The Samaritans had previously been shunned by the Jews when they offered to help build the temple of God (see Ezra 4:1-4). It becomes very evident that Sanballat, Tobiah, and the Samaritans do not want to see the Jews succeed at anything. Sanballat addresses his brethren, and the army of the Samaritans, regarding the building of the walls of Jerusalem. Apparently Sanballat was a high ranking officer of some sort in the Persian Empire and had the capability of demanding an ear by the Samaritan army. At first, Sanballat and Tobiah view the work on the wall as an impossible task and so they make fun of the workers. As they watch the work progress; however, they will feel the need to put an end to the work.

"**2** *And he spoke before his brethren and the army of Samaria, and said, What are these feeble Jews doing? Will they fortify themselves? Will they sacrifice? Will they make an end in a day? Will they revive the stones out of the heaps of rubbish, seeing they are burned? Now Tobiah the Ammonite was by him, and he said, Even that which they are building, if a fox go up, he shall break down their stone wall*" **(4:2).**

Sanballat's view of the Jews was that they were "*feeble*" and or pathetic. The objective of his speech to the Samaritan army is to muster them up to the same level of irritation that he has for the Jews. Sanballat accuses the Jews of trying to "*fortify*" the city of Jerusalem against the Persian Empire.

Sanballat, in a spirit of derision, mockingly said, 'What will they do, sacrifice in the morning and have the wall finished that night?' His comments indicate that the Jews have no idea as to the enormity of such a project and they may as well not even begin. Tobiah chimes in and says that even if they were able to build the wall it would be so insufficient that a fox's weight would cause it to crumble down. Sanballat and Tobiah do not believe that the Jews are capable of completing such a task not only due to their pathetic race but also because they don't have the material to do it.

The church of Jesus Christ often faces such derision and scorn today. Those who hate God's people have come up with many speeches to detour the conviction and spiritual progress of the saints. The wicked, found even within the Lord's church at times, have been heard saying, "Unity among so many people is impossible, no one can be perfect, no one can know all truth alike, there is no way anyone can meet the qualifications for elders outlined in 1 Timothy 3 so lets put in the next best thing, church discipline doesn't work, you can't be watchmen today that violates church autonomy, you can't convert people today because most people don't want to hear truth, and you can't possibly run the church today like it was run during the apostles' day. These are a few of the negative and pessimistic remarks that the haters of

God are saying yet there are Nehemiah's today that stand up and accomplish God's divine will.

"**4** *Hear, O our God; for we are despised: and turn back their reproach upon their own head, and give them up for a spoil in a land of captivity;* **5** *and cover not their iniquity, and let not their sin be blotted out from before you; for they have provoked you to anger before the builders*" **(4:4-5).**

Note that Nehemiah did not "*turn the other cheek*" in this incident. Someone today might remark that Nehemiah's prayer was hateful and that he was only practicing the same spirit that the Samaritans exercised toward them. What makes it right for Nehemiah to do so and not the Samaritans?

First, note that it was not Nehemiah, or any of the building Jews, who brought a quarrel to Sanballet and the Samaritans. Sanballet is the one who brought the ridicule and scorn to the building Jews. Under the Mosaic system it was an "*eye for an eye and tooth for tooth*" society. You do me wrong and I will be looking to do you wrong for payment. Sanballet's scorn hit deep within Nehemiah and caused him to pray a prayer of doom upon Sanballat and Tobiah. These two men did not represent the Lord of Host and so they were enemies. David is often found praying similar prayers in the Psalms regarding the enemies of God. As long as the wicked continued in their hardened state of sin there would be no forgiveness and neither would there be peace (see Psalms 58:6).

"**6** *So we built the wall; and all the wall was joined together unto half the height thereof: for the people had a mind to work*" **(4:6).**

We are not told how high the wall was to be; however, half the height was constructed. These seemingly feeble and foolish Jews were accomplishing the impossible in a short amount of time. When brethren have a "*mind to work*" there is no limit to the amount of good that can be accomplished. The Lord's church will be unified in

35

truth, organized with qualified elders, stand perfect before God, exercising discipline where necessary, knowledgeable of all truth, and converting the lost. While the pessimistic and unfaithful to God flounder around in their apathy the truth church of God is working and converting souls. Those with a "*mind to work*" and a proper view of the power of the gospel will accomplish much in the kingdom of God (Romans 1:16) (20l).

Nehemiah's enemies Response to seeing half of the Wall Completed (4:7-9)

"**7** *But it came to pass that, when Sanballat, and Tobiah, and the Arabians, and the Ammonites, and the Ashdodites, heard that the repairing of the walls of Jerusalem went forward, and that that the breaches began to be stopped, then they were very wroth;* **8** *and they conspired all of them together to come and fight against Jerusalem, and to cause confusion therein*" **(4:7-8).**

Jerusalem was surrounded by their enemies (The Samaritans to the North, Arabians to the South, Ammonites to the East, and Ashdodites to the West). Another power in the region would be unacceptable. Prejudice and hatred moved Sanballat and Tobaih to muster up the surrounding enemies of the Jews and form a coalition force to attack Jerusalem. To go to war over a wall illustrated the depth of the Jew's enemy's hatred for them. One thing the people of God find out in life is that for the most part we are always out numbered and surrounded (see Revelation 20:7-9). David said, "*I will not be afraid of ten thousands of the people that have set themselves against me round about*" as he called upon the Lord for deliverance from the multitude of his enemies (Psalms 3:6). Likewise the saints of God will always be outnumbered by the wicked (see Revelation 20:7-10). Those who put their trust in God will be victors now and forevermore over their enemies.

"**9** *But we made our prayer unto our God, and set a watch against them day and night, because of them*" **(4:9).**

Nehemiah and the working Jews gain intelligence of the purpose of their enemies. Two reactions are recorded: First, Nehemiah and the people pray to God and secondly they set up a watcher to warn them of the coming enemy. When the Christian faces the greatest difficulties in this life let us too watch and pray. Jesus said, "*Watch and pray that you enter not into temptation: the spirit indeed is willing but the flesh is weak*" (Mark 14:38).

The People Lose their Desire to build the Wall (4:10-14)

"**10** *And Judah said, The strength of the bearers of burdens is decayed, and there is much rubbish; so that we are not able to build the wall.* **11** *And our adversaries said, They shall not know, neither see, till we come into the midst of them, and slay them, and cause the work to cease.* **12** *And it came to pass that, when the Jews that dwelt by them came, they said unto us ten times from all places, You must return unto us*" **(4:10-12).**

The men doing the work on the wall were becoming exhausted. They looked around at all the trash and concluded that the task is just too great to accomplish. Furthermore there were rumors of the enemies attacking them and killing them so that the work of the wall would stop. Additionally, some of the Jews who lived by the neighboring enemies had heard that attacks were eminent and were encouraging the workers to return home before they were killed.

A shift in mentality has now taken place due to external circumstances. At the beginning of the work the people were excited and "*had a mind to work*" (Nehemiah 4:6). What happened to this initial zeal? Jesus tells us exactly what happens in the parable of the sower found at Matthew 13:18-23. Most are excited upon hearing and obeying the gospel of Jesus Christ. The first sign of tribulation and persecution; however, causes many to give up their faith. Still others permit the cares of this world to move them away from serving and obeying God's commands. The faithful; however, will not permit tribulation, persecution, or the cares of this world separate them from the love of God (see Romans 8:31-39). The Jews faith was put to the test and they failed to respond in trust. Thankfully, our merciful God gives man more chances and eventually they get back to work. Likewise, God is patient with us and when we fail to work we have more chances and opportunities to get it right (see 2 Peter 3:9).

"**13** *Therefore set I in the lowest parts of the space behind the wall, in the open places, I set there the people after their families with their swords, their spears, and their bows.* **14** *And I looked, and rose up, and said unto the nobles, and to the rulers, and to the rest of the people,* **Be not afraid of them**: *remember the Lord, who is great and terrible, and fight for your brethren, your sons, and your daughters, your wives, and your houses*" **(4:13-14).**

Nehemiah had delivered a motivational speech at Nehemiah 2:17-18, regarding building the wall, and the people responded by saying, "*let us rise up and build.*" Even after the discouraging words of derision delivered by Sanballat and Tobiah on two different occasions the people continued to work because they "*had a mind to work*" (Nehemiah 2:19 and 4:1-3). Exhaustion and fear now settle into their hearts and they are ready to quit.

Nehemiah responds to the people's dejected spirit by strategically placing the workers according to their families all around Jerusalem armed with weapons. Nehemiah then stands before the people and delivers a motivational speech of optimism and great faith. He encourages the people to rid themselves of the fear the enemies have caused to settle on their hearts. Secondly, Nehemiah tells the people to fight against their enemies remembering that God is with them, they have sons and daughters to protect, and they have their wives to think of and their property as well. Now is not the time to give up! There comes a time in every man's life when he must take a stand for what is right. Nehemiah is calling upon the people's faith that they may make that proper stand (16e).

Interestingly, we find similar, "*be not afraid of them*" statements or charges throughout the Bible. Moses repeatedly encouraged the Israelites to be fearless before their enemies. Moses writes, "*You shall not be afraid of them: you shall well remember what the Lord your God did unto Pharaoh and unto all Egypt*" (Deuteronomy 7:18). David said, "*In God have I put my trust, I will not be afraid; what can man do unto me?*" (Psalms 56:11) The prophet Isaiah writes, "*Behold, God is my salvation; I will trust, and will not be afraid; for Jehovah, even the Lord is my strength and song; and he is become my salvation*" (Isaiah 12:2). Jesus said, "*And be not afraid of them that kill the body but are not able to kill the soul: but rather fear him who is able to destroy both soul and body in hell*" (Matthew 10:28). The Apostle Paul writes, "*Finally, be strong in the Lord, and in the strength of his might. Put on the whole armor of God, that you may be able to stand against the wiles of the devil*" (Ephesians 6:10-11).

Nehemiah believed the wall project to be important enough to die for if necessary. The wall stood as a symbol of power and protection around the city of Zion. God had determined that it was to be built by his people. To build the wall of God's protection and defense was to put one's trust in God. The Lord would be a spiritual wall of fire around his saints who truly put their trust in him (see Zechariah 2:5).

The People respond to Nehemiah's Speech (4:15-23)

"**15** *And it came to pass, when our enemies heard that it was known unto us, and God had brought their counsel to naught, that we returned all of us to the wall, every one unto his work*" **(4:15).**

The results of Nehemiah's speech were immediate. The people respond by getting back to work. Nehemiah tells us that God had "*brought their counsel to naught*" but he doesn't give us any details. God had responded to the wicked enemies of the Jews by confusing them and not permitting them to organize a war against his people.

"**16** *And it came to pass from that time forth, that half of my servants wrought in the work, and half of them held the spears, the shields, and the bows, and the coats of mail; and the rulers were behind all the house of Judah.* **17** *They that built the wall and they that bare burdens laded themselves; ever one with one of his hands wrought in the work, and with the other held his weapon;* **18** *and the builders, every one had his sword girded by his side, and so built. And he that sounded the trumpet was by me*" **(4:16-18).**

Great **determination** is once again displayed in the people of God. They knew the dangers that were in front of them yet with their weapon in hand they continued to build.

What caused this motivation? While Nehemiah has brought out the obvious; i.e., they must protect their sons, daughters, and wives from the enemy, the primary reason the people are doing this work is because God has commanded it (see Ezra 6:14 and 9:9). We see the need to take a stand in truth today to protect our families and loved ones from being swayed by error. The underlying motivation; however, for our bold stand is that we too know that this is commanded of the Lord (Jude 3).

"**19** *And I said unto the nobles, and to the rulers and to the rest of the people, the work is great and large, and we are separated upon the wall, one far from another: in what place so ever you hear the sound of the trumpet, resort you there unto us; our God will fight for us*" **(4:19-20).**

Nehemiah makes a plan of action in case of attack. Due to the enormity of the wall project the people were scattered all over the city. Nehemiah tells the people to gather at his location if they hear the alarm trumpet sound and God would fight for them. There would be strength in numbers. When the saints of God are unified in truth and purpose there is no stopping their progress in knowledge and evangelizing the community.

"**21** *So we wrought in the work: and half of them held the spears from the rising of the morning till the stars appeared.* **22** *Likewise at the same time said I unto the people, Let every one with his servant lodge within Jerusalem, that in the night they may be a guard to us, and may labor in the day.* **23** *So neither I, nor my brethren, nor my servants, nor the men of the guard that followed me, none of us put off our clothes, every one went with his weapon to the water*" **(4:21-23).**

The wall project turned into a 24 hour a day affair. The work went on during the day and an overnight guard watched over the city during the night. Every one kept their weapon by their side. The chance of attack was real yet the people continued to work. There was never a moment that they could let their guard down. The enemy was real yet they knew that God was on their side.

Questions over Nehemiah Chapter 4

1. **True or False:** Sanballat and Tobiah were confident that the Jews would complete the wall around Jerusalem.

2. **True or False:** Nehemiah and the working Jews were unaware that they were being mocked?

3. Why type of mind did the Jews have that brought them success?

4. Who determined to fight against Jerusalem and cause the work on the wall to come to a halt?

5. Why did the people of God stop working on the wall around Jerusalem?

6. Why did Nehemiah say that there was no need to fear the Samaritans, Arabians, Ammonites, and Ashdodites?

7. Why did the construction workers that labored at the wall of Jerusalem have weapons attached to them?

NEHEMIAH CHAPTER 5

Synopsis

Discouragement has always been a very effective tool of the devil. The people of God were discouraged by the antagonism toward them and their work yet they pressed on to the work of God (Nehemiah chapter 4). Nehemiah chapter five reveals heightened levels of discouragement in the form of poverty, hunger, and broken homes. The wall working Jews were being forced to mortgage their lands, vineyards, homes, and even their children in slavery so that they could eat and pay their taxes without halting the wall construction. One would think that it was the ungodly who were taking advantage of the wall workers in their time of need yet it was the nobles and rulers of God's people (shepherds) (see Nehemiah 5:7).

A similar event happened during the days of the prophet Ezekiel. The prophet of God explains that it was the duty of the shepherds (nobles and rulers of Israel) to keep the people encouraged and ready to serve. The shepherds; however, created an environment of discouragement and failure. Ezekiel exposes the wickedness of the shepherds saying, "4 *The diseased have you not strengthened, neither have you healed that which was sick, neither have you bound up that which was broken, neither have you brought back that which was driven away, neither have you sought that which was lost; but with force and with rigor have you ruled over them*" (Ezekiel 34:4). The nobles and rulers of Jerusalem, in the days of Nehemiah, had also ruled with force and rigor.

Application

The Lord's people of all ages need to be encouraged to keep doing the work of the Lord. Shepherds (elders, deacons, and preachers) can be very helpful when encouraging their fellow Christians to keep the faith. Christians in a local setting must remember their unity and fellowship in Christ and put their hands as one to the plow of edifying the saints, teaching the lost, and providing benevolence to needy saints (John 17:20-21 and Ephesians 4:1-16) (22a). The prophets and apostles, though doing God's ordained work, were not immune to discouragement. Paul needed the encouragement of the Lord (Acts 23:11 and 2 Timothy 4:17). Paul made request to the Ephesians saints that they may pray for him to not cower down when he needed to be bold and say the necessary things to people (see Ephesians 6:19-20). If we will remember the relationship we have as fellow saints, along with our common spiritual work, we will see to it that we help each other every step of our lives (see Acts 2:44-47; 4:32-37 and 1 Peter 2:17). The wealthy of Jerusalem would have done well to sell their own lands and give to their needy brethren. Nehemiah wanted to be remembered by God as one who loved and cared for his brethren rather than loving the riches of this world (Nehemiah 5:19). Sometimes spiritual work must take precedence over our own personal responsibilities. When the work is done we may get caught up on all else that has been lacking. God's work must always take priority in our lives!

Nehemiah 5

A financial depression sets in due to the hard work of building the walls of Jerusalem (5:1-5)

"**1** *Then there arose a great cry of the people and of their wives against their brethren the Jews.* **2** *For there were that said, We, our*

44

sons and our daughters, are many: let us get grain, that we may eat and live" **(5:1-2).**

The wall project took priority over all else in life. The people worked on the wall in the day time and slept within the walls during the night. Consequently, no one was able to go to their farms to work and make wages to pay their every day expenses. Some of their own brethren were taking the wall project as an opportunity to get gain from the workers. Seems odd how some wait for disaster to hit and find a way to profit from those affected by the tragedy yet so is the wicked world we live in.

"3 Some also there were that said, We are mortgaging our fields, and our vineyards, and our houses: let us get grain, because of the dearth" **(5:3).**

The problem of hunger sets in and the people do what is necessary to gain grain to eat. The workers were not being paid for the work on the wall. The hungry people found themselves in the desperate position of having to mortgage their fields, vineyards, and houses for grain. A dilemma arises among the people of God. The command to build is taken very serious yet the people had personal needs at the same time. The workers had been so diligent that they neglected even their health.

"4 There were also that said, We have borrowed money for the king's tribute upon our fields and our vineyards. 5 Yet now our flesh is as the flesh of our brethren, our children as their children: and, lo, we bring into bondage our sons and our daughters to be servants, and some of our daughters are brought into bondage already: neither is it in our power to help it; for other men have our fields and our vineyards" **(5:4-5).**

The lack of money presented very real and difficult situations for the convicted Jews who were working on the wall. The people kept the command of God to build the wall to the detriment of their own financial well being. Not only had many of the people mortgaged their homes, fields, and vineyards for grain but they had borrowed money to pay tribute tax to the Persian Empire. Some had even gone so far as having to sell their sons and daughters as slaves to meet their financial obligations. The wall project was draining the people of God of their wealth and putting a strain on their families.

Nehemiah responds to the news of Hunger, Tribute, and Slavery (5:6-13)

"**6** *And I was very angry when I heard their cry and these words.* **7** *Then I consulted with myself, and contended with the nobles and the rulers, and said unto them, You exact usury, every one of his brother. And I held a great assembly* **against them**" **(5:6-7).**

When Nehemiah heard of the people mortgaging their homes, fields, and vineyards to feed themselves while they worked he was very angry. Nehemiah could not believe that some people were even selling their children as bondservants to pay tribute to the Persians. Rather than rashly lashing out in anger the man of God takes a moment to meditate on the matter and then he speaks out. Nehemiah accuses the "*nobles and the rulers*" of Jerusalem with exacting "*usury*" against their own brethren. To take a fellow brother's house, field, vineyard, sons and daughters at a time of his deep crises is a depraved and unloving thing to do. Nehemiah calls all the people to attend a "*great assembly*" and the people were "*against*" the nobles and rulers for their wickedness.

"**8** *And I said unto them, We after our ability have redeemed our brethren the Jews, that were sold unto the nations; and would you even sell your brethren, and should they be sold unto us? Then held they their peace, and found never a word*" **(5:8).**

Nehemiah addresses the great assembly that was against the nobles and rulers of Jerusalem. Nehemiah reminds the rulers and nobles that they had been sold into Babylonian bondage and redeemed by

God. Do the rulers and nobles dare take captive again those that God released? Do the rulers and nobles take God's law into their own hand and fearlessly exact "*usury*" against the will of God (see Exodus 22:25; Leviticus 35:ff and Deuteronomy 23:19). The rulers and nobles remained silent as Nehemiah spoke.

"**9** *Also I said, the thing that you do is not good:* **ought you not to walk in the fear of our God,** *because of the reproach of the nations our enemies?*" **(5:9).**

The Common English Bible reads, "*So I continued, 'What you are doing isn't good! Why don't you walk in the fear of our God? This will prevent the taunts of the nations that are our enemies!*" The sin of the rich was that they did these things not to help their brethren in time of need, as was the lawful design of loans and selling a daughter or son into slavery under the Mosaic Law, but they did these things for self gain. Their loveless actions were a manifestation of a lack of "*fear*" toward God in their lives.

Throughout the Bible we find commands to "*fear God.*" The law of God instructs man to fear him yet the hard of heart want no part of God's ways (see Proverb 15:33). Solomon defines fearing God as departing from and hating evil (Proverbs 3:7). Solomon further defines the fear of God as pride, arrogance, perverse speech, and evil ways in general (Proverbs 8:13). Fearing God means walking uprightly according to the laws of righteousness and justice (Proverbs 14:2). Those who fear God are those who have reverence and respect for the authority of God's laws (Colossians 3:17). Those who fear God are the meek and lowly who put God's laws and paths before their own personal opinions, convictions, and consciences. No man in his right mind would dare not fear Jehovah God (2 Peter 2:10-12). The wall workers were putting their fear of God before their own personal needs yet were being taken advantage of.

The command to fear God is a similar command to "believe or have faith God" (see Hebrews 11:6). The Bible tells us that it is the one who "*believes*" that will be saved (Acts 16:30-31 and Romans 10:11-13). The "belief" or "faith" under consideration is not a verbal proclamation only but rather a life of obedience that makes manifest one's true faith and belief. A study of the book of Acts puts this in clear perspective. Throughout the book of Acts one's faith and obedience are used synonymously. Follow the progression of thoughts starting with the believers that were baptized for the forgiveness of their sins at Acts 2:38-44 and moving to the obedient believers at Acts 4:4; 5:14; 6:7; 8:12-13; Acts 10:42-43; 13:38-39; 14:1-2 see also Mark 16:16 and Hebrews 11:1ff. Both Jesus (John 3:36) and the apostles (Romans 1:5) taught that man's faith is manifest in his works of obedience. Likewise, one's fear of God is manifest in his actions of obedience to God's commandments (36). To say that we love Jesus is to obey Jesus (John 14:15). To say that we know God is to obey God (1 John 2:4-5). To say that we love our brethren is to obey God's commands (1 John 5:1-4). God knows what is manifest in our hearts by our outward actions (Matthew 7:15-16).

Nehemiah warns the rulers and nobles that their actions will bring the reproach of the nations against Jerusalem and her efforts to build the wall. God is never with the wicked yet he will fight for the righteous.

"**10** *And I likewise, my brethren and my servants, do lend them money and grain. I pray you, let us leave off this usury.* **11** *Restore, I pray you, to them, even this day, their fields, their vineyards, their olive yards, and their houses, also the hundredth part of the money, and of the grain, the new wine, and the oil, that you exact of them*" **(5:10-11).**

The Bible in Basic English reads, "10 *Even I and my servants have been taking interest for the money and the grain we have let them have. So now, let us give up this thing.*" Nehemiah and his servants had been doing the same things that the rulers and nobles of Jerusalem are guilty of. Nehemiah was apparently lending money to the working Jews that were hungry and needed money to pay their taxes to the Persian Empire. The man of God has opened his eyes to this great error and demanded that he, the rulers, and nobles all restore the working people's homes, vineyards, fields, and children of bondage. He also demands that the *"hundredth part of the money"* be restored to them (this was evidently the amount of interest charged on the loans).

"12 Then said they, We will restore them, and will require nothing of them; so will we do, even as you say. Then I called the priests, and took an oath of them, that they would do according to this promise" **(5:12).**

Nehemiah stands before the rulers and nobles of Jerusalem with a great assembly that is against them for taking advantage of them at a time of great need. The scene must have been awesomely fearful to the nobles and rulers. Not only had they violated God's laws in this matter but they were starring down the eyes of some weary and angry Jews that had been cheated. The rulers and nobles are not going to deny such a request in the sight of all the people they had exacted usury against. They all, with one accord, decide to return all that they had taken from their brethren in their time of need. Nehemiah seals the deal by calling upon the priests of God to serve as witnesses to the oath made by the rulers and nobles.

"13 Also I shook out my lap, and said, So God shake out every man from his house, and from his labor, that performs not this promise; even so be he shaken out, and emptied. And all the assembly said, Amen, and praised Jehovah. And the people did according to this promise" **(5:13).**

Secondly, Nehemiah confirms the oath by a symbolical act of shaking his garments. An oath has been made before God and witnessed by the priests of the Lord. The people's homes, vineyards, and fields would now be restored to them by way of this oath.

Nehemiah's Good Character Revealed (5:14-19)

"**14** *Moreover from the time that I was appointed to be their governor in the land of Judah, from the twentieth year even unto the thirty second year of Artaxerxes the king, that is, twelve years, I and my brethren have not eaten the bread of the governor*" **(5:14).**

Nehemiah sounds like a wealthy business man. He had offered loans for interest to his fellow working Jews yet he did not take a salary from them as their governor (Nehemiah 5:10). Nehemiah's term as governor over Jerusalem and Judah lasted a total of 12 years (see introduction). During these years he never once "*ate the bread of the governor.*"

"**15** *But the former governors that were before me were chargeable unto the people, and took of them bread and wine, besides forty shekels of silver; yea, even their servants bare rule over the people: but so did not I,* **because of the fear of God**" **(5:15).**

The former governors had taken wages from the people, however, Nehemiah had not due to great "*fear of God.*" Fearing God equates to keeping his commandments (see Ecclesiastes 12:13). Nehemiah could not take money as wages from the people while they suffered hunger and the emotional pains of having their children sold as slaves. Nehemiah had plenty of money and to charge Israel interest for loans would be ungodly.

When God's people have plenty they ought to be content rather than trying to get more and more. The Apostle Paul tells us that the love of money is a root of all kinds of evils (see 1 Timothy 6:10). The love of money moved the nobles and rulers of Jerusalem to practice usury. The love of money moved the nobles and rulers to heartlessly take the wall workers' sons and daughters as slaves. Nehemiah would not participate in these things. Though Nehemiah has much of these worlds' goods he will not lower himself to greater gains at the expense of those who have very little. The "*fear of God*" moved Nehemiah to share his wealth rather than cheating the poor to gain more and more. The inference is that taking advantage of the poor to get greater gains is not "*fearing God*" (25h).

"**16** *Yea, also I continued in the work of this wall, neither bought we any land: and all my servants were gathered here unto the work*" **(5:16).**

Not only did Nehemiah, as governor of the land for twelve years, not charge interest or take people's lands for exchange of food but he also labored right along side them on the wall project. Nehemiah did not consider himself above getting his hands dirty with his brethren (30x).

"**17** *Moreover there were at my table, of the Jews and the rulers, a hundred and fifty men, besides those that came unto us from among the nations that were round about us.* **18** *Now that which was prepared for one day was one ox and six choice sheep; also fowls were prepared for me, and once in ten days store of all sorts of wine: yet for all this I demanded not the bread of the governor, because the bondage was heavy upon this people.* **19** *Remember unto me, O my God, for good, all that I have done for this people*" **(5:17-19).**

Nehemiah regularly fed the 150 heads of Jewish households at his own expense. He never took a salary as their governor. He did the work because he loved God and his people. This is what Nehemiah wanted to be remembered for by God. Though the governor had taken interest on loaned money in the past he has rejected this practice as of now. Nehemiah's prayer is that God would remember his good deeds among the people as they labored on the wall.

Nehemiah Chapter 5 Questions

1. What had the working Jews done to eat grain and pay their taxes?

2. What was Nehemiah's reaction to the people's acts of desperation?

3. **True or False:** Nehemiah was not guilty of charging the people interest on their loans for food and the necessities of life.

4. Who was responsible for exacting usury on the working Jews?

5. Discuss the *"fear of God"* and how it relates to the events of Nehemiah chapter 5.

6. What caused the rulers and nobles to restore all that they had taken from the working Jews?

7. **True or False:** Nehemiah had never taken wages from the Persian Empire or the Jews for standing in as their governor.

8. How long had Nehemiah been governor over the land of Judah to this point of our study?

9. What did Nehemiah want God to remember about him?

NEHEMIAH CHAPTER 6

Synopsis

Just when Nehemiah and the wall working Jews may have felt that the worst of their troubles were past they face new troubles. News of the wall's completion has created heightened passions of hatred. Sanballat and Tobiah, and to Geshem the Arabian seek the life of Nehemiah. These wicked men believed that if only they could destroy Nehemiah they would finally stop the Godly progress of the Jews. Jealousy, hatred, and anger govern the hearts of the wicked and they will stop at nothing to have their way. Nehemiah and wall working Jews' biggest test comes in the form of Tobiah's relationships within the ranks of God's people. Family and friendships are strong ties that often cannot be broken even by divine truths. Many people's hearts are quickly hardened when God's word demands uniformity even from family and friends.

Application

A lesson that is gradually coming out in this study is the persistence of the wicked against the righteous. There is an old saying, "There is no fury like that of a woman that has been scorned." We may coin another similar phrase as follows: "There is no fury among men like that of a wicked man exposed for what he truly is." The wicked will seek out revenge and attempt to keep their foot over the neck of the righteous so that their guilt may be soothed. Jesus tells us several times that he and his apostles tell us all these things before they happen so that we may not become discouraged (see John 16:1 etc.). If God's people would take knowledge of the Lord's warnings we would be less likely so easily discouraged. Too often we let little things discourage us from doing the work of the Lord yet if we will look to the example of men like Nehemiah maybe we would all toughen up a bit. There are not many of us that have faced threats to our lives due to our faith (see Hebrews 12:4).

Those who hate the saints and love the riches, fame, and lust of this world fall flat on their face now and forevermore (see Revelation 18:1-3). Though the wicked number as the sand of the sea they shall fall at the hands of the living God (Revelation 20:7-10). True victory belongs to the saints of every generation (1 Corinthians 15:57-58). We must not give up (Hebrews 10:32-39)! We must not fail! We must keep pressing forward knowing that God is with us (Romans 8:31ff). The people of God complete the wall in fifty two days because they had a mind to work. Imagine the good work the saints and church today can accomplish if brethren are united in their mind to work.

Nehemiah 6

Sanballat, Tobiah, and Geshem try to lure Nehemiah out of the City (6:1-4)

"**1** *Now it came to pass, when it was reported to Sanballat and Tobiah, and to Geshem the Arabian, and unto the rest of our enemies, that I had built the wall, and that there was no breach left therein (though even unto that time I had not set up the doors in the gates),* **2** *that Sanballat and Geshem sent unto me saying, Come, let us meet together in one of the villages in the plain of Ono. But they thought to do me mischief*" **(6:1-2).**

The wall was now complete and the only remaining work to be done was on the doors and gates. The impressive work did not go unnoticed. The enemies of the Jews had gained word that the wall was nearing completion and once again it turned them to anger. Such is the world we live in. As Christians live their lives in godliness and do the work of the church it will always anger the wicked. The Apostle Paul wrote, "12 *All those who live Godly in Christ Jesus will suffer persecution*" (2 Timothy 3:12). Jesus said, "18 *If you are hated by the world, keep in mind that I was hated by the world before you*" (Common English Bible John 15:18). If Nehemiah and the people of God would have shared in a hatred of progress for the kingdom of God then they would have been received with open arms by the Samaritans, Sanballat, Tobiah, and Geshem the Arabian. If only God's people would reject his divine commandment to build the wall they would have been accepted by the people around them (Ezra 6:14; 9:9 and Nehemiah 2:17). Again, Jesus said, "19 *if you belonged to the world, the world would love you as its own. However, I have chosen you out of the world, and you don't belong to the world. This is why the world hates you*" (Common English Bible John 15:19).

Sanballat, Tobiah, and Geshem the Arabian attempt to lure Nehemiah out of the city's protective walls that they might do "*mischief*" to him. These men were not merely frustrated (Nehemiah 4:2) but they were murderously angry (Nehemiah 4:7-8). The enemies of the Jews were ready to kill Nehemiah for his part in leading them to rebuild the city walls. Throughout the history of God's people and the early church the enemies of God have fostered an intense hatred for the saints. The enemies of God wanted killed Stephen as he spoke words of truth and exposed the dark hearts of the wicked (Acts 7:51-60). The enemies of God wanted Paul dead because he rejected their religious ideology of Jewish laws and preached the resurrection of Jesus and the forgiveness of sins (see Acts 14:19). The enemies of God killed Stephen as he was calling out to God (Acts 7:51-60). The wicked killed Jesus as he took their sins to the cross. Jesus said, "1 *these things have I spoken unto you, that you should not be cased to stumble. 2 They shall put you out of the synagogues: yea, the hour comes that whosoever kills you shall think that he offers service unto God*" (John 16:1-2).

As long as the saints of God have a mind to work in spiritual matters there will be workers of Satan to do all within their power to stop it. Satan has a passionate hatred for the saints of God and seeks to destroy them every chance he gets (see Revelation 12:13-17). The wicked will never rest as they are convicted of sin by the righteous. Their pride and arrogance will not permit the righteous to have any advantage over them.

"**3** *And I sent messengers unto them, saying, I am doing a great work, so that I cannot come down: why should the work cease, while I leave it, and come down to you?* **4** *And they sent unto me four times after this sort; and I answered them after the same manner*" **(6:3-4).**

Nehemiah answers his enemies request by stating that he will not come to them because he involved in a "*great work*." Four times Sanballat, Tobiah, and Geshem write letters to Nehemiah trying to lure him out of the city and each time Nehemiah replies that he is too busy doing the work of the Lord.

The "*great work*" of Bible people is spiritual (see John 18:36). Nehemiah would not permit poverty, hunger, discouragement, or personal responsibilities to stand in the way of this God ordained work (see chapter 5 above). Nehemiah, like the later Apostle Paul, labors with vigor to accomplish the work of God (see 1 Corinthians 15:10). May it be that modern day Christians see these examples in the Old and New Testaments and keep our hands to the plow as we labor in the kingdom of God. Never are we to permit the workers of wickedness to discourage us or move us from our God ordained work.

"**5** *Then sent Sanballat his servant unto me in like manner the fifth time with an open letter in his hand,* **6** *wherein was written, it is reported among the nations, and Gashmu said it, that you and the Jews think to rebel; for which cause you are building the wall: and you would be their king, according to these words.* **7** *And you have also appointed prophets to proclaim about you at Jerusalem, saying, There is a king in Judah: and now shall it be reported to the king according* to these words.   Come now therefore, and let us take council together" **(6:5-7).**

Sanballat, after four failed attempts to get Nehemiah out of the city, writes a fifth *"open letter."*   The objective of the enemies of Nehemiah has obviously remained the same.   They wanted to assassinate Nehemiah and end the revitalization of the city they hated so much.   Nehemiah has made a noticeable difference in the city of Jerusalem and the Samaritans want this progress stopped.

The open letter would be assessable to all to read and know its contents.   Sanballat and his fellows were openly charging Nehemiah with rebellion against the Medo-Persian Empire.   Secondly, they charged that Nehemiah was spreading word by the prophets that he was to be king of Judah.   Sanballat writes that he is reporting these rumors to Artaxerxes and that Nehemiah needs to come out of the city to talk these charges over.   No doubt it would have been very tempting to Nehemiah to clear the air regarding this matter yet the governor of Judah knows that Sanballat is a hateful and murderous man that cannot be trusted.

"**8** *Then I sent unto him, saying, There are no such things done as you say, but you invent them out of your own heart.* **9** *For they all would have made us afraid, saying, Their hands shall be weakened from the work, that it be not done.   But now, O God, strengthen my hands"* **(6:8-9).**

Nehemiah wisely replies to Sanballat's open letter with another letter of his own rather than appearing in person.   The governor of Jerusalem and Judah rejects the accusations as being lies *"invented out of the heart"* of Sanballat.   The Bible in Basic English reads for Nehemiah 6:9, *"For they were hoping to put fear in us, saying, Their hands will become feeble and give up the work so that it may not get done.   But now, O God, make my hands strong."*   Sanballat and his hateful buddies were willing to go to any length to stop the progress of the Jews in Jerusalem.

Likewise, many wicked men today go through great lengths to discredit and destroy a faithful brother in Christ who has convicted them of sin. Once one has been exposed as a sinner they would often rather retaliate rather than repent. One thing we note from Nehemiah chapters two through six is that God's enemies are persistent (see Luke 4:13 and 1 Peter 5:8-9). Sanballat and his coconspirators have plotted in anger against Nehemiah and the Jews from the beginning of the wall project (Nehemiah 2:19), at the midway point (Nehemiah 4:1-3), end of the wall project (Nehemiah 6:1ff), and even after the wall was completed (see later at Nehemiah 6:19).

The tactics of the enemies of God's people have been to **question Nehemiah's motives** for doing a good work (Nehemiah 2:19 as compared to 2 Corinthians 12:16-18 when some of the Corinthians similarly questioned Paul about collecting money for needy saints). Secondly, the enemies of God's people use scorn and mocking tactics to discourage and strike fear into the people (Nehemiah 2:19 as compared to the Romans mocking and spitting on Jesus - Matthew 27:29-31 and Luke 18:32 and the calling of derogatory names such as when Paul was called an "idiot" at 2 Corinthians 11:5). Thirdly, the enemies of God's people use other tactics such as **discouragement** (Nehemiah 4:1-3), **threats** (Nehemiah 4:11), **craft and deceit** (Nehemiah 6:1-4 as compared to 2 Corinthians 2:11 and 4:1-2), **false accusations** (Nehemiah 6:5-8 as compared to Mark 15:3 and Acts 26:2) and **intimidation of fear** (Nehemiah 6:9, 13, 19 and 2 Timothy 1:7) (8c).

The Christian's response to the persistent vises of the wicked is to be strengthened in the Lord through truth (Psalms 61:7-8; Ephesians 3:16 and 6:10). Nehemiah responds to the wicked vices of Sanballat by saying, "*I am doing a great work, so that I cannot come down*" (Nehemiah 6:3). Like Jesus we too must learn not to give the wicked the time of day. Let the people of God today defeat the wicked with **conviction** (Nehemiah 2:20; 6:9; 1 Corinthians 4:9-13 and 2 Timothy

3:6-8), **Courage** (Nehemiah 4:14; 6:11 and Acts 7:51), **prayer** (Nehemiah 4:4, 9 and 1 Thessalonians 5:17-18), and **determination** (Nehemiah 4:6 and Philippians 3:13-14). God's people are to **expose** the plans of the wicked (Nehemiah 5:6-7; 6:8 and Ephesians 5:11) and **ever be cautious** of the evil workers that may be within the church (Nehemiah 6:10ff compared to 2 Peter 2:1ff).

Sanballat and Tobiah try another stratagem to discredit Nehemiah (6:10-14)

"**10** *And I went unto the house of Shemaiah the son of Delaiah the son of Mehetabel, who was shut up; and he said, let us meet together in the house of God, within the temple, and let us shut the doors of the temple: for they will come to slay you; yea, in the night will they come to slay you.* **11** *And I said, Should such a man as I flee? And who is there, that, being such as I, would go into the temple to save his life? I will not go in.* **12** *And I discerned, and, lo, God had not sent him; but he pronounced this prophecy against me: and Tobiah and Sanballat had hired him*" **(6:10-12)**.

Tobiah and Sanballat hire a false prophet, Shemaiah, to seduce Nehemiah into going into the holy place of God's temple to seek protection from advancing assassins. Nothing further is known of this prophet Shemaiah other than it is a testament of evil working from within the people of God. The next two verses reveal him to be like the nobles and rulers of Jerusalem along with Balaam of old who loved the hire of money (see 2 Peter 2:15; Jude 1:11 and Revelation 2:14).

Tobiah and Sanballat had once again plotted the demise of Nehemiah. Nehemiah knew that he was not authorized to enter the holy place (see Numbers 18:7). If Nehemiah did this, his enemies would have occasion to spread the news of his unlawful deed. We see the unscrupulousness of their actions and for modern false teachers as well. They should have seen by this time that Nehemiah was a man of faith and would in no way fall for such a destitute plan.

Nehemiah figured this out quickly. What kind of prophet of God would tell him to violate God's commandments?

"**13** *For this cause was he **hired**, that I should be afraid, and do so, and sin, and that they might have matter for an evil report, that they might reproach me.* **14** *Remember, O my God, Tobiah and Sanballat according to these their works, and also the prophetess Noadiah, and the rest of the prophets, that would have put me in fear*" **(6:13-14).**

Nehemiah knew that such an act of entering the temple would be a matter of "*sin*." Tobiah and Sanballat figured that if they could have Nehemiah charged with sin then the people would lose confidence in him and the wall project would go undone. Nehemiah is viewed as the head of the snake. If only Sanballat and Tobiah could cut his head off they would not have problems out of the Jews.

Nehemiah again prays to God. His prayer is that God would remember these wicked attempts to cause him to sin that the walls of Jerusalem would go undone. Who would like to be in Sanballat and Tobiah's shoes on judgment day? Jesus said, "*Whosoever shall cause one of these little ones that believe on me to stumble, it is profitable for him that a great millstone should be hanged about his neck, and that he should be sunk in the depth of the sea*" (Matthew 18:6).

Consider the efforts of the wicked to kill the wall around Jerusalem project. God's people have been mocked and ridiculed by the wicked (Nehemiah 2:19 and 4:2-3). The wicked have discouraged the workers by taking their lands, vineyards, homes, and even sons and daughters (chapter 5). The wicked have attempted to kill Nehemiah with schemes of trickery (Nehemiah 6:1-4). The wicked have tried to trip up Nehemiah in lies (Nehemiah 6:5-7). The wicked have attempted to get Nehemiah to sin so that they may have a matter against him (Nehemiah 6:10-14). All the efforts of the wicked have failed to accomplish their goal of killing the wall project because Nehemiah and the people had a "*mind to work*" (Nehemiah 4:6).

A great lesson is learned from this Old Testament book. The wicked, of every generation, will fail at destroying the true church and individual saints. Though the odds are against God's people the wicked will fail miserably. We learn this lesson from the book of Revelation. Those who hate the saints and love the riches, fame, and lust of this world fall flat on their face now and forevermore (see Revelation 18:1-3). Though the wicked number as the sand of the sea they shall fall at the hands of the living God (Revelation 20:7-10). True victory belongs to the saints of every generation (1 Corinthians 15:57-58). We must not give up (Hebrews 10:32-39)! We must not fail! We must keep pressing forward knowing that God is with us (Romans 8:31ff).

The wall is completed (6:15-16)

"**15** *So the wall was finished in the twenty and fifth day of the month Elul, in fifty and two days*" **(6:15).**

Fifty two days is a little over a month and a half. Consider the fact that Nebuchadnezzar first takes captives from Judah when Jehoiakim was king and Jeremiah's prophecy, regarding 70 years of captivity, begins. Daniel was among the first captives. Twenty years latter Zedekiah is attacked by Nebuchadnezzar and Judah is utterly conquered. Nebuchadnezzar destroys the city of Jerusalem and its walls at that time taking many more captives. The walls were destroyed twenty years into the seventy years of captivity. Additionally, at the time of Nehemiah coming on the scene it had been ninety years since Cyrus had permitted Zerubbabel to return with the captives to rebuild the temple of God. The walls had lain destroyed and in ruins for 140 years! It is amazing to now see that it only took 52 days to rebuild it at a grueling pace.

The difference in these times is very significant. God's people should have completed the wall many years ago yet they permitted discouragement and fear to rule their hearts. When the Lord's people have a "*mind to work*" there are great things that can be accomplished (see Nehemiah 4:6). Think about all the years that go by in a local work where there is little to no growth, no elders, no deacons, and sometimes a complete disintegration of a local church. Think what could and should have been done if only the brethren had a "*mind to work*" (20I). Too many times we are all too busy with our own lives of school, work, and recreation to take the time to do the laborious work of evangelizing the world. Jesus said, "*The harvest indeed is plenteous but the laborers are few: pray therefore that the Lord of harvest would send forth laborers into his harvest*" (Luke 10:2). It matters not if we are contemplating the work of personal evangelism, benevolence to needy saints, or edification of church members we must be about the work of the Lord if we expect to see results. Though the Jews and Nehemiah were greatly plagued with the hatred of the enemies they worked diligently. No matter the level of discouragement we must press on in the work of God!

"**16** *And it came to pass, when all our enemies heard thereof, that all the nations that were about us feared, and were much cast down in their own eyes; for they perceived that this work was wrought of our God*" **(6:16).**

Knowledge of Jehovah God existed in the hearts of the other nations. The surrounding nations considered God's hand to be in the work when it was completed. How could such a great task under such deflating circumstances happen over fifty two days without divine help? The result of such diligent and faithful work was that God was glorified and his enemies put to shame.

More Difficulties (6:17-19)

"**17** *Moreover in those days the nobles of Judah sent many letters unto Tobiah, and the letters of Tobiah came unto them.* **18** *For there were many in Judah sworn unto him, because he was the son-in-law of Shecaniah the son of Arah; and his son Jehohanan had taken the daughter of Meshullam the son of Berechiah to wife*" **(6:17-18).**

The word "*moreover*" indicates an additional difficulty that Nehemiah would have to deal with. Nehemiah not only faced opposition to doing God's work from outside the ranks of saints but within as well (see also Nehemiah 6:10-14). Tobiah was being informed by the nobles of Judah regarding the state of affairs. Tobiah presented somewhat of a difficult problem for Nehemiah. He was related **to Shecaniah** who was the keeper of the East gate (Nehemiah 3:29). Shecaniah's family had come to Jerusalem with Ezra (Ezra 8:3). He was a spokesmen for those who had sinned against God's marriage laws and repented (Ezra 10:2). He and his family worked side by side with other Jews in restoring the walls (Nehemiah 3:29). Secondly, **Tobiah was also related to Berechiah** (another worker on the wall / see Nehemiah 3:4, 30). Latter we read that **Tobiah was allied to Eliashib the priest** (Nehemiah 13:4). Here was an individual with strong inside relationships. This would not be a problem if Tobiah was a decent and godly man; however, he was anything but decent and holy. Remember that Tobiah has been "*exceedingly grieved*" that Nehemiah was repairing the wall around Jerusalem (Nehemiah 2:9-10). He has publicly laughed (Nehemiah 2:19), mocked (Nehemiah 4:2), and threatened to fight Nehemiah and the Jews for building the walls (Nehemiah 4:7-8). Tobiah has plotted to kill Nehemiah by luring him out of the walled city (Nehemiah 6:1-2). When that didn't work he sought to have Nehemiah's name destroyed by tempting him to illegally go into the temple of God for shelter from those who would kill him (Nehemiah 6:10-12).

Tobiah's inner relationships with family, friends, and nobles of Judah make him a difficult problem. He was like a cancer in the house of God. Nehemiah knew that Tobiah was not a good man yet to get Judah to see their spiritual duty he had to work along side this wicked man. How could Nehemiah rid Judah and Jerusalem of such a wicked man without loosing the people's faith and respect? Often times there are very wicked men in the church that are causing issues due to a desire to have preeminence among the brethren (see 3 John 9). These wicked men have family and friends in the church that make dealing with them difficult. The true faithful must find a way to rid the church of this troubling influence lest they form solid factions and overthrow the godly ones.

"**19** *Also they spoke of his good deeds before me, and reported my words to him. And Tobiah sent letters to put me in fear*" **(6:19).**

Nehemiah just finished a hard fought battle against the enemies of God so that the walls would be complete. The wall was God's objective for his people (again see Ezra 6:14). Now, many rulers of the Jews actively supported Tobiah simply because of their relationship to him. The rulers spoke well of Tobiah in the hearing of Nehemiah and reported anything said by Nehemiah to Tobiah. Tobiah would respond by writing threatening letters to Nehemiah that he may be "*put in fear.*"

Some of the Lord's people could not see through their relationship with Tobiah because of their hard hearts. They elevated their family and friends above God and greatly erred. Many in the church today will gladly exercise church discipline on anyone; however, when their family member is affected they throw the word of God to the wind. Jesus said, "*A man's foes shall be they of his own household*" (Matthew 10:36). Likewise, many have no problem identifying a false teacher yet when that false teacher is their son, father, or mother you can forget it. Their blood relationship is more important to them than their relationship with God. Jesus said, "37 *He that loves his father or mother more than me is not worthy of me; and he that loves his son or daughter more than me is not worthy of me*" (Matthew 10:37). Where will you be standing when your son, daughter, father, mother, nephew, or niece teaches or practices error? May God give us all the conviction and faith to stand with the Lord.

Questions over Nehemiah Chapter 6

1. What did Sanballat and Geshem do to try to get Nehemiah out of the city?

2. What did Sanballat's "*open letter*" accuse Nehemiah of?

3. What did the false prophet Shemaiah try to do to Nehemiah?

4. How long did it take Nehemiah and the Jews to complete the wall?

5. **True or False:** Tobiah had inside relationships with the people of God.

6. What problems has Tobiah caused so far for the people of God building the wall?

7. What lessons can we learn from Nehemiah's persistent work ethic in the face of many discouraging events?

8. What do we learn about the persistence of the wicked?

NEHEMIAH CHAPTER 7

Synopsis

Nehemiah has successfully moved his kindred to complete the wall around Jerusalem. The time for him to honor his pledge to Artaxerxes, regarding returning to his post as the king's cup bearer, has arrived. Nehemiah's desire is to leave the people in good spiritual standing. He appoints two God fearing men to take his place. Nehemiah also gathers the people, by divine order, and makes an official account of their genealogy so that no one is found serving in the place of a priest that should not be there (Nehemiah 7:64). The people are so excited about the day's events that many give of their own wealth into the treasury of God. The people were now safe and confident in God and his ability to help them.

Application

Nehemiah's good character continues to surface. The governor could have rebelled against Artaxerxes and remained in Jerusalem yet he kept his word. He chooses God fearing men to replace him. He fulfills God's command to establish an official genealogy of the people. His objective, like all of ours ought to be, was the welfare of the people of God.

Nehemiah 7

Nehemiah Prepares to Return East to the Persian Empire so that he may Resume his Duties as Cup Bearer to the King (7:1-7)

"**1** *Now it came to pass, when the wall was built, and I had set up the doors, and the porters and the singers and the Levites were appointed,* **2** *that I gave my brother Hanani, and Hananiah the governor of the castle, charge over Jerusalem; for he was a faithful man, and feared God above many*" **(7:1-2)**.

Nehemiah had accomplished what he set out to do in fifty two days. He had promised Artaxerxes that he would return to his duties as cup bearer after the wall was completed and so he is ready to honor that pledge (see Nehemiah 2:6).

Nehemiah hands over all civil authority in Jerusalem to his brother Hanani (see Nehemiah 1:2) and Hananiah the governor of the castle. The qualification for these two men serving in the place of Nehemiah is their "*fear of God.*" A lack of God's fear before the eyes of the shepherds (i.e., nobles and rulers of Jerusalem) was the reason for Nehemiah's condemning speech found at chapter 5:9-12. Jerusalem and Judah needed God fearing men to lead the city and nation from this point forward.

"**3** *And I said unto them, Let not the gates of Jerusalem be opened until the sun be hot; and while they stand on guard, let them shut the doors, and bar them: and appoint watches of the inhabitants of Jerusalem, every one in his watch, and every one to be over against his house.* **4** *Now the city was wide and large; but the people were few therein, and the houses were not built*" **(7:3-4)**.

Extra precautions were to be made by the inhabitants of Jerusalem. They had been threatened and were not to take this lightly (see Nehemiah 4:11). Nehemiah instructs them to not open the gate until the "*sun is hot*" and to keep it shut all night with bars. Watchmen were to ever be on the walls. Though the city was wide and large there were only a few residents. Their houses remained in ruins and there was much work to do. All of these types of statements help us to envision the extent that Nebuchadnezzar laid waist the city some 140 years earlier. It also tells us how that the people of God left off their own interest for the construction of the wall. Such a spirit had not always been in the people of God (see Haggai 1:1-4).

"5 And my God put into my heart to gather together the nobles, and the rulers, and the people, that they might be reckoned by genealogy. And I found the book of the genealogy of them that came up at the first, and I found written therein: 6 These are the children of the province, that went up out of the captivity of those that had been carried away, whom Nebuchadnezzar the king of Babylon had carried away, and that returned unto Jerusalem and to Judah, every one unto his city; 7 who came with Zerubbabel, Jeshua, Nehemiah, Azariah, Raamiah, Nahamani, Mordecai, Bilshan, Mispereth, Bigvai, Nehum, Baanah. The number of the men of the people of Israel:" **(7:5-7).**

God communicated with Nehemiah by way of inspiration (see Galatians 1:11-12 and 2 Peter 1:21). The Lord inspired or moved Nehemiah to make an official record of the people's genealogy. The significance of this was related to the temple service and spiritual work of each individual within the kingdom of God. Those who were not in the lineage of Aaron were not to be priest. Even those in the lineage of Aaron were to be subdivided, according to the Mosaic Law, to perform various tasks in and around the temple.

Nehemiah *"found the book of genealogy of them that came up at the first."* A record had been made of all the Jews who returned with Zerubbabel to rebuild the temple of God (see Ezra 2 and 7). Nehemiah repeats the list with a few differences from the Ezra account. Nehemiah assembled the people and Ezra was to read the Law of Moses to them all (Nehemiah 8:1ff).

A List of all who originally returned under the leadership of Zerubbabel (7:8-73)

Consider the following registry from Nehemiah 7:8-67:

- *The children of Parosh, two thousand a hundred and seventy and two.*

- *The children of Shephatiah, three hundred seventy and two.*

- *The children of Arah, six hundred fifty and two.*

- *The children of Pahath-moab, of the children of Jeshua and Joab, two thousand and eight hundred [and] eighteen.*

- *The children of Elam, a thousand two hundred fifty and four.*

- *The children of Zattu, eight hundred forty and five.*

- *The children of Zaccai, seven hundred and threescore.*

- *The children of Binnui, six hundred forty and eight.*

- *The children of Bebai, six hundred twenty and eight.*

- *The children of Azgad, two thousand three hundred twenty and two.*

- *The children of Adonikam, six hundred threescore and seven.*

- *The children of Bigvai, two thousand threescore and seven.*

- *The children of Adin, six hundred fifty and five.*

- *The children of Ater, of Hezekiah, ninety and eight.*

- *The children of Hashum, three hundred twenty and eight.*

- *The children of Bezai, three hundred twenty and four.*

- *The children of Hariph, a hundred and twelve.*

- *The children of Gibeon, ninety and five.*

- *The men of Bethlehem and Netophah, a hundred fourscore and eight.*

- *The men of Anathoth, a hundred twenty and eight.*

- *The men of Beth-azmaveth, forty and two.*

- *The men of Kiriath-jearim, Chephirah, and Beeroth, seven hundred forty and three.*

- *The men of Ramah and Geba, six hundred twenty and one.*

- *The men of Michmas, a hundred and twenty and two.*

- *The men of Beth-el and Ai, a hundred twenty and three.*

- *The men of the other Nebo, fifty and two.*

- *The children of the other Elam, a thousand two hundred fifty and four.*

- *The children of Harim, three hundred and twenty.*

- *The children of Jericho, three hundred forty and five.*

- *The children of Lod, Hadid, and Ono, seven hundred twenty and one.*

- *The children of Senaah, three thousand nine hundred and thirty.*

- *The priests: The children of Jedaiah, of the house of Jeshua, nine hundred seventy and three.*

- *The children of Immer, a thousand fifty and two.*

- *The children of Pashhur, a thousand two hundred forty and seven.*

- *The children of Harim, a thousand [and] seventeen.*

- *The Levites: the children of Jeshua, of Kadmiel, of the children of Hodevah, seventy and four.*

- *The singers: the children of Asaph, a hundred forty and eight.*

- *The porters: the children of Shallum, the children of Ater, the children of Talmon, the children of Akkub, the children of Hatita, the children of Shobai, a hundred thirty and eight.*

- *The Nethinim: the children of Ziha, the children of Hasupha, the children of Tabbaoth, the children of Keros, the children of Sia, the children of Padon, the children of Lebana, the children of Hagaba, the children of Salmai, the children of Hanan, the children of Giddel, the children of Gahar, the children of Reaiah, the children of Rezin, the children of Nekoda, the children of Gazzam, the children of Uzza, the children of Paseah. The children of Besai, the children of Meunim, the children of Nephushesim, the children of Bakbuk, the children of Hakupha, the children of Harhur, the children of Bazlith, the children of Mehida, the children of Harsha, the children of Barkos, the children of Sisera, the children of Temah, the children of Neziah, the children of Hatipha.*

- *The children of Solomon's servants: the children of Sotai, the children of Sophereth, the children of Perida, the children of Jaala, the children of Darkon, the children of Giddel, the children of Shephatiah, the children of Hattil, the children of Pochereth-hazzebaim, the children of Amon.*

- *All the Nethinim, and the children of Solomon's servants, were three hundred ninety and two.*

- *And these were they that went up from Tel-melah, Tel-harsha, Cherub, Addon, and Immer; but they could not show their fathers' houses, nor their seed, whether they were of Israel:*

- *The children of Delaiah, the children of Tobiah, the children of Nekoda, six hundred forty and two. And of the priests: the children of Hobaiah, the children of Hakkoz, the children of Barzillai, who took a wife of the daughters of Barzillai the Gileadite, and was called after their name. These sought their register among those that were reckoned by genealogy, but it was not found: therefore were they deemed polluted and put from the priesthood. And the governor said unto them, that they should not eat of the most holy things, till there stood up a priest with Urim and Thummim.*

The "Urim and Thummim" was "a means of revelation used by the high priest in giving Yahweh's answer to inquires" (ISBE volume 4, page 957). Apparently there was no current high priest available to stand before God with these emblems to find the truth of the matter of a man's genealogy. There was; however, plans to soon have this take place.

"**66** *The whole assembly together was forty and two thousand three hundred and threescore,* **67** *besides their men-servants and their maid-servants, of whom there were seven thousand three hundred thirty and seven: and they had two hundred forty and five singing men and singing women*" **(7:66-67).**

A total of around 50,000 people returned with Zerubbabel (see Ezra chapter 2 for a comparison).

"**68** *Their horses were seven hundred thirty and six; their mules, two hundred forty and five;* **69** *their camels, four hundred thirty and five; their asses, six thousand seven hundred and twenty*" **(7:68-69).**

There are minor discrepancies in the numbers as compared with Ezra two. This is especially so with the numbers of material and supplies given in these two verses (1d). Number discrepancies should never cause one to question the validity of God's word (see Romans 1:18-19). Through the process of time this document was kept preserved.

"**70** *And some from among the heads of fathers' houses gave unto the work. The governor gave to the treasury a thousand darics of gold,* *fifty basins, five hundred and thirty priests' garments.* **71** *And some of the heads of fathers' houses gave into the treasury of the work twenty thousand darics of gold, and two thousand and two hundred pounds of silver.* **72** *And that which the rest of the people gave was twenty thousand darics of gold, and two thousand pounds of silver, and threescore and seven priests' garments.* **73** *So the priests, and the Levites, and the porters, and the singers, and some of the people, and the Nethinim, and all Israel, dwelt in their cities. And when the seventh month was come, the children of Israel were in their cities"* **(7:70-73).**

The wall was now complete. The temple of God had been restored. Ezra had restored the people to spiritual fellowship and service to God. The functions of God's kingdom were now to proceed in God's divine order. So excited were many of the people that they gave to the common treasury of the city gold, silver, and priestly garments.

Nehemiah had gained permission from Artaxerxes to come to Jerusalem and build the city walls during the first month of the Hebrew calendar (Nisan) (see Nehemiah 2:1). It was in the seventh month (Tishri) of that same year that Nehemiah found the genealogies and gathered the people together.

Questions over Nehemiah Chapter 7

1. Who did Nehemiah place in charge of Jerusalem?

2. Why didn't Nehemiah stay and govern the people he loved?

3. Why did Nehemiah gather the nobles, rulers, and people of Judah together?

4. How many people had returned to Jerusalem with Zerubbabel?

NEHEMIAH CHAPTER 8

Synopsis

Consider the following time frame of the book of Nehemiah:

Nehemiah is introduced at the twentieth year of Artaxerxes during the month Chislev (Ninth Hebrew month) (Nehemiah 1:1)

Nehemiah gains permission to return to Jerusalem to rebuild the city's walls during the month Nisan of Artaxerxes' twentieth year (First Hebrew month) (Nehemiah 2:1)

Nehemiah reveals that he served a total of twelve years as governor in Jerusalem from the twentieth year of Artaxerxes to the thirty second year (Nehemiah 5:14). Examining this time frame helps us see that he must have remained in Jerusalem for eleven years after the wall was completed.

Nehemiah and the Jews complete the wall project in 52 days during the month Elul (sixth Hebrew month) (Nehemiah 6:15).

The people are all within the protected walls of Jerusalem in the seventh month (Tishri) (Nehemiah 7:73).

All the people are gathered to hear the law read on the first day of the seventh month (Nehemiah 8:2).

The people make a public confession of their sins on the twenty fourth day of the seventh month (Nehemiah 9:1ff).

Nehemiah returns to Artaxerxes as his cup bearer in the thirty second year of the king's reign (Nehemiah 13:6).

Nehemiah chapter eight records the historical event of Ezra reading the law of God in the hearing of the people. The priest of God read for approximately six hours without a break. Nehemiah tells us that the people were attentive, respectful, interested, and then grieved. The excitement of the moment turned to sorrow as they listened with honest hearts and saw their sins laid before them. There were things in God's laws, such as keeping the Feast of Tabernacles, which they were not even aware of.

Application

The disposition of respect, attentiveness, and reverential interest in the word of God is a formula for spiritual success in people of all ages. When the word of God is opened and read people discover their shortcomings. The word of God pierces deep within a man's soul and demands adjustments (see Hebrews 4:12). When God's word is actually read it will bring hope and joy to those who comply with its standards. Others will experience a heart throbbing agony of grief as they discover their own sins. The exposure of one's sins will move the honest to Godly sorrow and repentance (see 2 Corinthians 7:8-10). Those who refuse to open the Bible for themselves and read it; however, will be forever confused and misled.

Nehemiah 8

Ezra Reads the Law of Moses to the People (8:1-8)

"**1** *And all the people gathered themselves together as one man into the broad place that was before the water gate; and they spoke unto Ezra the scribe to bring the book of the law of Moses, which Jehovah had commanded to Israel*" **(8:1).**

75

The remnant of God's people assembled at the request of God by the mouth of Nehemiah so *"that they might be reckoned by genealogy"* (Nehemiah 7:5). The time was the *"seventh month"* (Nehemiah 7:73b). Chapter six left us at the Hebrew month Elul (the sixth month of the twentieth year of Artaxerxes) (Nehemiah 6:15). The wall was now complete after 52 days of intense labor and stress from the enemies. The location of their gathering was near the water gate (southeast of the temple). While assembled, the people speak unto Ezra requesting that the Law of Moses be read to them. It is probable that the reason for this request was their faith in God's providential care and help in the wall building project. Though many years had passed they now were successful in rebuilding the temple and the city walls as well as restoring the people spiritually. There was, at this time, a heightened sense of accomplishment in relationship to God's laws. Ezra was viewed by the people as a man who represented the law and so they ask him to read it in their hearing.

*"**2** And Ezra the priest brought the law before the assembly, both men and women, and all that could hear with understanding, upon the first day of the seventh month. **3** And he read therein before the broad place that was before the water gate **from early morning until midday**, in the presence of the men and the women, and of those that could understand; and the **ears of all the people were attentive** unto the book of the law"* **(8:2-3).**

Where has Ezra been throughout this study? Apparently Ezra has remained in Judea for the past 20 years and took no real important part in rebuilding the wall (at least that is recorded). Ezra reads the Law of Moses in the hearing of all the people from *"early morning until midday"* (possibly six hours). While Ezra read the people were *"attentive"* unto the Laws of God. The miraculous completion of the wall in 52 days was an obvious sign that God was with them. God had their attention and, for the time being, their interest in the laws of God has been revived. When people are perceptive of God's work in their lives they are generally moved to be more religious. People of the world find themselves more interested in God around Christmas and Easter times yet when those holidays are past they are back to the old grind of immorality. Our objective as Christians is to always see God's grace and mercy in our lives.

"**4** *And Ezra the scribe stood upon a pulpit of wood, which they had made for the purpose; and beside him stood Mattithiah, and Shema, and Anaiah, and Uriah, and Hilkiah, and Maaseiah, on his right hand; and on his left hand, Pedaiah, and Mishael, and Malchijah, and Hashum, and Hashbaddanah, Zechariah, and Meshullam. 5 And Ezra opened the book in the sight of all the people (for he was above all the people); and when he opened it, all* **the people stood up**" **(8:4-5).**

A pulpit of wood was prepared for Ezra and this special occasion that elevated him above all the people so that they could all see him. To Ezra's right were six priests and to his left were seven. Ezra approaches the pulpit in the sight of the people and opens the books of the law. Upon opening the books all the people stood upon their feet probably as a show of respect and reverence for the Word of God. The stage is set for the people to hear and understand God's laws. They are both attentive and reverential to God's words. These two qualities are a formula for good understanding within the heart of man.

"**6** *And Ezra blessed Jehovah, the great God; and all the people answered Amen, Amen, with the lifting up of their hands: and they* **bowed their heads***, and worshipped Jehovah with their faces to the ground*" **(8:6).**

An act of worship occurs here on the part of the people. Ezra blesses the name of Jehovah God and the people respond by saying, Amen, Amen while lifting their hands. Secondly, the people respond to the event by bowing their faces to the ground in humble submission to the Lord. More and more characteristics of reverence, fear, and determination to do right are detected in the people.

"**7** *Also Jeshua, and Bani, and Sherebiah, Jamin, Akkub, Shabbethai, Hodiah, Maaseiah, Kelita, Azariah, Jozabad, Hanan, Pelaiah, and the Levites,* **caused** *the people to understand the law: and the people* **stood in their place.** **8** *And they read in the book, in the law of God, distinctly; and they gave the sense, so that they understood the reading*" **(8:7-8).**

Apparently Ezra would read some of the law and priests and Levites would give an interpretation or explanation. The people were left with a clear understanding of the law of God. The Common English Bible reads as follows for verse 8: "*They read aloud from the scroll, the Instruction from God, explaining and interpreting it so the people could understand what they heard.*" Explanation and interpretation of Bible text has ever been a duty to perform for congregational edification. While the prophets and priests did this in the Old Testament days we have preachers and elders in New Testament days (Acts 8:30-31 and Romans 10:14-15) (18c).

The People Respond to the Reading of the Law of God (8:9-12)

"**9** *And Nehemiah, who was the governor, and Ezra the priest the scribe, and the Levites that taught the people, said unto all the people, this day is holy unto Jehovah your God; mourn not, nor weep. For* **all the people wept, when they heard the words of the law**" **(8:9).**

Nehemiah, Ezra, and the Levites tell the people that this is a holy day unto Jehovah because much good has come of it. The people, however, are deeply grieved and wept after hearing the Law of God read. No doubt Ezra read sections of the law that exposed their sin and the punishing consequences thereof. They heard God's warnings and saw that the state that they were in was due to their sins and their fathers before them. This response indicates a heart that was not only willing to hear and understand but to act. The people's sins bothered them. Without this response to the gospel truths there will be no conversion (see 2 Corinthians 7:8-10).

"**10** *Then he said unto them, Go your way, eat the fat, and drink the sweet, and send portions unto him for whom nothing is prepared; for this day is holy unto our Lord: neither be grieved; for the joy of Jehovah is your strength.* **11** *So the Levites stilled all the people, saying, Hold your peace, for the day is holy; neither be grieved.* **12** *And all the people went their way to eat, and to drink, and to send portions, and to make great mirth, because they had understood the words that were declared unto them*" **(8:10-12).**

Jewish feasts, as revealed in the Mosaic Law, were designed to bring joy not sadness (see Deuteronomy 12:7). Nehemiah encourages the people to remove their sadness and participate in a joyous feast unto Jehovah God. A great swing of emotions occurs. The people begin with heavy hearts over their exposed wickedness yet are moved to joy over the prospect of God's mercy. Nehemiah also encourages the wealthier people to provide a feast for the poorer among them that all may be joyous.

Celebration of the Feast of Tabernacles (8:13-18)

"**13** *And on the second day were gathered together the heads of fathers houses of all the people, the priests, and the Levites, unto Ezra the scribe, even to give attention to the words of the law.* **14** *And they found written in the law, how that Jehovah had commanded by Moses, that the children of Israel should dwell in booths in the feast of the seventh month;* **15** *and that they should publish and proclaim in all their cities and in Jerusalem saying, Go forth unto the mount, and fetch olive branches, and branches of wild olive, and myrtle branches, and palm branches, and branches of thick trees, to make booths, as it is written*" **(8:13-15).**

The heads of the fathers' houses assembled together with Ezra the next day for further inquiry of the Mosaic Law. Upon close examination, they found that they were to be keeping the Feast of Booths or Tabernacles at this time of year. By the reading of verse 14 it appears as though they read this and were surprised. It appears that their prior knowledge of the feast of Tabernacles must have driven them to seek out the particulars of this feast. So they endeavor to study with Ezra, the priest, over the matter.

As they studied the Law, they found that the whole congregation was to participate in erecting booths of branches to dwell in on the fifteenth day of the seventh month for seven days (see Leviticus 23:39-43). While it may surprise us that God's people had obviously not been keeping his set feasts we might want to look to our present day. Scores of people today have no clue as to what day to worship God on (i.e., the day to sing, pray, preach, give of our means, and partake of the Lord's Supper). When the Book of Law is not opened it is not known. There have been other times in the history of God's people when God's word was found, read, and discoveries about the people's negligence is discovered. Every generation of mankind must find it within their hearts to open the word of God and read it rather than letting it be a decoration upon a bookshelf or coffee table (19a).

"**16** *So the people went forth, and brought them, and made themselves booths, every one upon the roof of his house, and in their courts, and in the courts of the house of God, and in the broad place of the water gate, and in the broad place of the gate of Ephraim.* **17** *An all the assembly of them that were come again out of the captivity made booths, and dwelt in the booths: for since the days of Jeshua the son of Nun unto that day had not the children of Israel done so. And there was very great gladness*" **(8:16-17).**

The results of their research and resolve to comply are impressive. The whole congregation obeyed and kept the feast of Tabernacles making themselves booths of branches and dwelling in them for seven days. These were days of restoration. So impressive was the universal keeping of this feast that the inspired writer records, "*for since the days of Joshua the son of Nun unto that day had not the children of Israel done so.*" One problem with this statement is that at 2 Chronicles 7:9 and 1 Kings 8:65 we find recorded the people of God keeping the feast of Tabernacles after the dedication of Solomon's temple. Then again, we read in Ezra 3:4 that the people kept the feast of Tabernacles. The explanation is a simple one yet impressive. Since the days of Israel entering into Canaan, God's people as a whole had not kept the feast of Tabernacles. Obviously bands of people did throughout the years, however, here we find the whole congregation submitting to this law. Those who open the word of God, read it, and respond will find favor with God.

While it may be our tendency to lay blame at Ezra's feet (i.e., why didn't he initiate this sooner??) let us remember that he was but one man and that which brought all Israel together was the miraculous completion of the wall around Jerusalem in 52 days. God had his hand in these events (Nehemiah 7:5). A national gathering gave way to an opportunity to reunite the people of God as one and to restore spiritual laws and goals in the minds of the people. No doubt the promises of God through the Messiah were revisited and the people have a renewed hope.

"**18** *Also day by day from the first day unto the last day, he read in the book of the law of God. And they kept the feast seven days; and on the eighth day was a solemn assembly, according unto the ordinance*" **(8:18).**

Ezra reads the Law of Moses for eight straight days in the hearing of all the people. This chapter reveals a renewed interest in spiritual service to God on the part of the people. It is fascinating to note the power of God's word upon the minds of men. Often times people are very hungry for the truth yet do not know where to find it. Once the Bible is opened, read, and explained they are infused with interest in serving God. The Apostle Paul said, "*For I am not ashamed of the gospel: for it is the power of God unto salvation to every one that believes; to the Jew first, and also to the Greek*" (Romans 1:16). We may convert more people today if we have the opportunity to open God's laws and read them to the public. Christians today ought to be searching out ways to do this. Far too many denominational people and those who do not attend church desperately need to hear the word of God so that they may fear, obey, and then rejoice as did the people in the days of Nehemiah and Ezra (19n).

Questions over Ezra Chapter 8

1. Where did the people assemble?

2. What did the great assembly request of Ezra?

3. What did all the people do when Ezra opened the book of the Law?

4. What was the people's response to Ezra blessing the name of God?

5. Why did the people weep and feel grief as the law of God is read?

6. Why did the people make "*booths*?" (tents or temporary housing)

7. How long had it been since Israel had done this?

8. **True or False:** The word of God is powerful enough to turn the greatest sinners to Christ.

NEHEMIAH CHAPTER 9

Synopsis

Great fear comes over the people of God as they hear the Law of Moses read. The more they hear the more they see the necessary changes in their lives. The people of God had joined themselves to the wicked in the world to the point that there were no distinguishing characteristics to tell who was who (see also Psalms 106:34-36). Israel was also guilty of marrying foreigners that God had commanded not to do. Thirdly, they had profaned the Sabbath day. The people remedy the situation by separating themselves from the wicked so that they may serve God as a unit in fellowship with God and each other. The word of God had cut directly to their heart as it was designed by God to do (see Hebrews 4:12). At this point it is most probable that Ezra stands before the people and prays on their behalf to God.

Israel's hearts were filled with guilt and needed reformation. God's priest prays on behalf of the broken hearted people who were in sin. The prayer may be subdivided into five parts. First, Ezra prays regarding the singularity and might of Jehovah God (Nehemiah 9:6-8). Secondly, Ezra prays in regards to God's hand being with the Hebrews who came up out of Egypt and received the laws at Sinai (Nehemiah 9:9-15). The third part of Ezra's prayer considers the forty years that Israel wandered through the wilderness of sin and learned many valuable, yet costly, lessons (Nehemiah 9:16-23). The forth division of

Ezra's prayer examines God blessing Israel with the land promise of Canaan (Nehemiah 9:24-31). The fifth part of Ezra's prayer is a confession of public sins and an appeal to God's care and history with his people that he may be merciful to them (Nehemiah 9:32-38).

Application

The Apostle Paul told the Corinthians that godly sorrow works repentance (see 2 Corinthians 7:8-10). When people open their Bibles today and read the instructions of God they too will be convicted of sin. The contrite and meek of the earth will comply with God's commandments and purpose to conform their lives to the image of Jesus Christ (Romans 8:29). The duty of God's people in every age is to not only read the Bible for their own spiritual welfare but to encourage others to read it as well. The more we read the more we will learn and be drawn to God (see John 6:44-45). God's powerful word will cut through us as a sword and cause guilt, shame, and great sorrow over our sins (Romans 1:16 and 3:23).

As we read the prayer of Ezra we find beautiful and unchanging characteristics of God. When we step away from the deity of Jehovah we find just the opposite with Israel. The people of God were fearful, inconsistent in their fear and obedience of God, and unyielding in their hardened state of mind. Though God had done so much for them throughout their history they continued to rebel. The more they rebelled; however, the more God justly chastised them. God is not willing that any should perish (2 Peter 3:9). We learn from this section that God is merciful and will strike those who persist in wickedness only that they may repent (Revelation 16:8-11). God continues to work the same way today. Those who reject his mercy and love are chastised with the hope of correcting them to repentance (Hebrews 12:3-13). Let us all open our eyes to God's love and mercy and obey his commandments (Romans 6:15-23).

Nehemiah 9

The people assemble again in Jerusalem to make Confession of Sins (9:1-5)

"**1** *Now in the twenty and fourth day of this month the children of Israel were assembled with fasting, and with sackcloth, and earth upon them.* **2** *And the seed of Israel separated themselves from all foreigners, and stood and confessed their sins, and the iniquities of their fathers.* **3** *And they stood up in their place, and read in the book of the law of Jehovah their God a fourth part of the day; and another fourth part they confessed, and worshipped Jehovah their God*" **(9:1-3).**

Just two days after the feast of Tabernacles the people once again assemble at the temple for reading of the law, worship, confession of sin, and prayer. What is impressive about this assembly is that it was on a day when they were not required to do so by law. They were simply worshipping due to their sincere love of God and desire of his mercy in light of their past sin. The reading of the law had convicted them of their sins and their hearts were heavy knowing the judgments of God. The Jews made a show of their great sorrow for sins committed by fasting, putting sackcloth on, and had the earth on them from casting it into the air as a show of grief. These reactions illustrated hearts that were truly bothered by their sin. A great power of God's word is that it is able to cut into the heart of a man and fill him with great guilt and sorrow. The meek of the earth recognize God's high expectation of holiness and are grieved when they do not achieve this (Matthew 5:48; Romans 3:20-21; 1 Peter 1:15-16; 2 Peter 1:4; 1 John 4:17 etc.). Godly sorrow over sins moves one to repentance (see 2 Corinthians 7:8-10).

The use of the word "*seed*" illustrates the connection of the Jews to Abraham as a family of spiritual commonality. The Jews, after reading the laws of God on fellowship, saw that they were unlawfully joined with unbelievers. They had lost their sanctification in that they could not be distinguished from those of the world. When the Christian today dresses, talks, and acts like the sinful of the world they are no longer viewed as faithful to God (see 2 Corinthians 6:14-7:1).

The people worshipped and read the law of God for about four to six hours and then spent the same amount of time confessing both their own sins and the sins of their fathers. The people's hearts were determined to be completely right with God. The Mosaic Law demanded absolute perfection from the Jews yet offered no remedy for any failures (see Galatians 3:10 and Hebrews 7:18-19). The distinct difference (Romans 3:21-22) between the Law of Moses and the "*law of faith*" (Romans 3:27) is that people can be forgiven through faith in Jesus.

"*Then stood up upon the stairs of the Levites, Jeshua, and Bani, Kadmiel, Shebaniah, Bunni, Sherebiah, Bani, and Chenani, and cried with a loud voice unto Jehovah their God*" (9:4).

These men may have been heads of their families who were seeking mercy from God after hearing the word of the Lord. These men "*cried with a loud voice*" as they sought to be heard by the Lord. Nehemiah chapter nine illustrates hearts moved by godly sorrow over sins. These people were bothered by the fact that they had not met God's expectations. The only way people will change from sinful lives to lives of righteousness today is to identify their error and be bothered by it (14m).

"**5** *Then the Levites, Jeshua, and Kadmiel, Bani, Hashabneiah, Sherebiah, Hodiah, Shebaniah, and Pethahiah, said, stand up and bless Jehovah your God from everlasting to everlasting; and blessed be your glorious name, which is exalted above all blessing and praise*" **(9:5).**

Eight Levites stand praising God before the assembly. The word "*bless*" here indicates an expression of great honor bestowed upon God on the part of the prayers. The admonition of the Levities is that the people "*bless Jehovah*" or show him reverence and fear by purposing to follow his commandments. The entire event demonstrated the people's great fear of God. They knew, by reading the Law of Moses, that they were guilty and they did not want to face God's wrath.

Ezra's Prayer (9:6-38)

"**6** *You are Jehovah, even you alone; you have made heaven, the heaven of heavens, with all their host, the earth and all things that are thereon, the seas and all that is in them, and you preserve them all; and the host of heaven worships you.* **7** *You are Jehovah the God, who did choose Abram, and brought him forth out of Ur of the Chaldees, and gave him the name of Abraham,* **8** *and found his heart faithful before you, and made a covenant with him to give the land of the Canaanite, the Hittite, the Amorite, and the Perizzite, and the Jebusite, and the Girgashite, to give it unto his seed, and you have performed your words; for you are righteous*" **(9:6-8).**

Ezra begins by confessing the identity and creative power of God. The prophet Isaiah wrote, "*Remember the former things of old: for I am God, and there is none else; I am God, and there is none like me*" (Isaiah 46:9). God proves his deity to man in that he made the heavens and its hosts, earth, and the sea. The evidences of God's being are too obvious to ignore and all those who do stand without excuse before the Almighty creator of heaven and earth (see Romans 1:20).

Furthermore, God providentially chose Abraham to bring his seed promise to the world. God "*found*" that Abraham was "*faithful.*" God put Abraham to the test and when the patriarch passed the Lord said, "*For now I know that you fear God*" (Genesis 22:12). God granted Abraham his blessed promises "*because*" Abraham obeyed his commandments (Genesis 22:16-18 as well as 26:4-5). The Apostle Paul tells us that all today are justified by the same obedient faith that Abraham had long ago (see Romans 4). To look to God's identity and creation is sufficient to put hope into the hearts of all men.

"**9** *And you saw the affliction of our fathers in Egypt, and heard their cry by the Red Sea,* **10** *and showed signs and wonders upon Pharaoh, and on all his servants, and on all the people of his land; for you knew that they dealt proudly against them, and did get you a name, as it is this day.* **11** *And you did divide the sea before them, so that they went through the midst of the sea on the dry land; and their pursuers you did cast into the depths, as a stone into the mighty waters.* **12** *Moreover in a pillar of cloud you led them by day; and in a pillar of fire by night, to give them light in the way wherein they should go.* **13** *You came down also upon mount Sinai, and spoke with them from heaven, and gave them right ordinances and true laws, good statutes and commandments,* **14** *and made known unto them your holy Sabbath, and commanded them commandments, and statutes, and a law, by Moses your servant,* **15** *and gave them bread from heaven for their hunger, and brought forth water for them out of the rock for their thirst, and commanded them that they should go in to possess the land which you had sworn to give them*" **(9:9-15).**

The second part of Ezra's prayer looks at God helping the Hebrews out of Egypt. Ezra acknowledges God's watchful eyes that were over the Hebrews as they served under cruel bondage to the Egyptians. Moses writes, "12 *the more they afflicted them, the more they multiplied and the more they spread abroad. And they were grieved because of the children of Israel*" (Exodus 1:12). The Lord eventually uses Moses to deliver the people from their bondage. God performed great wonders and signs as he plagued Egypt to show his great might and power (see Romans 9:17).

The power of God was witnessed first hand by the Egyptian army as they pursued the Hebrews into the Red Sea and were consumed by the walls of water. God greatly cared for his people on that occasion and many more to come. Ezra remembered how God guided them through the desert by a pillar of cloud by day and fire by night

(Deuteronomy 6:11). Ezra recalls how that God spoke to the people causing them to fear his Almighty name at Sinai and he gave them the Law (see Exodus 20:20). Furthermore, God cared for his people by raining manna from heaven and giving them water to drink from a rock. God's gracious care was with his people and his command for them was that they go and take possession of the land of Canaan as he had promised to Abraham.

God's love and care for Israel is depicted in this section of Ezra's prayer. The prophet Isaiah said, "7 *I will make mention of the lovingkindnesses of Jehovah, and the praises of Jehovah, according to all that he has bestowed on us, and the great goodness toward the house of Israel, which he has bestowed on them according to this mercies, and according to the multitude of his lovingkindnesses. 8 For he said, Surely, they are my people, children that will not deal falsely: so he was their Savior. 9 In all their affliction he was afflicted, and the angel of his presence saved them: in his love and in his pity he redeemed them; and he bare them, and carried them all the days of old*" (Isaiah 63:7-9). God continues to love, protect, guard, and guide his people today (see Zechariah 9:8, 15; 1 Peter 1:1, 5:2:9, and 10). Israel of old and spiritual Israel today remains the apple of his eye (Zechariah 2:8).

"**16** *But they and our fathers dealt proudly, and hardened their neck, and did not give heed to your commandments,* **17** *and* **refused to obey, neither were mindful of your wonders** *that you did among them, but hardened their neck, and in their rebellion appointed a captain to return to their bondage.* **But you are a God ready to pardon, gracious and merciful, slow to anger,** *and abundant in lovingkindness, and forsook them not.* **18** *Yea, when they had made them a molten calf, and said, this is our God that brought us up out of Egypt, and had wrought great provocations;* **19** *yet in your manifold* **mercies** *you forsook them not in the wilderness: the pillar of cloud departed not from over them by day, to lead them in the way; neither the pillar of fire by night, to show them light, and the way wherein* *they should go.* **20** *You gave also your good Spirit to instruct them, and withheld not your manna from their mouth, and gave them water for their thirst.* **21** *Yes, forty years did you sustain them in the wilderness, and they lacked nothing; their clothes waxed not old, and their feet swelled not.* **22** *Moreover you gave them kingdoms and peoples, which you did allot after their portions: so they possessed the land of Sihon, even the land of the king of Heshbon, and the land of Og king of Bashan.* **23** *Their children also multiplied as the stars of heaven, and you brought them into the land concerning which you did say to their fathers, that they should go in to possess it"* **(9:16-23).**

The third part of Ezra's prayer is from verse 16 to 23. Ezra reviews what transpired as the people of God wandered in the wilderness for forty years due to their disobedience. Many lessons are learned from this period. God had cared for his people and commanded them to take Canaan yet they rebelled against his divine will. Ezra acknowledges the sin of those in the wilderness wanderings as twofold. These two cases of sinful behavior reveal a common denominator of the people exchanging God's commandments for something that they wanted (see Romans 1:25). A hard heart is defined as doing one's own will rather than the will of God (14f).

First, the people sinned in that they "*hardened*" their hearts against God's commandments. God instructed his people to march to Canaan and take possession of the land. Canaan was a land flowing with milk and honey, however, when the people saw how great the enemy appeared they concluded that they were but grasshoppers in their sight (Numbers 13:33). The people began to murmur and then sought to appoint a captain to lead them back to Egypt to serve in bondage (Numbers 14:1-5). They had a greater fear of man than they did of God. Their trust in God took a backseat to their immediate fears. Though God had done so much for them they could not see past the immediate perceived dangers. Their minds were blinded by fear and they rejected the Almighty. Though God had performed great wonders before their eyes they were not "*mindful*" of his glory and neither did they obey him. The Apostle Paul described the Romans of his day in similar language. Paul said that the Gentiles "*refused*" to have God in their knowledge even though he was revealed to them in the creation (see Romans 1:20, 25, 28).

Secondly, God had instructed the people not to worship idols (Exodus 20:1-4) and yet they set aside God's instructions when they built the calf in the wilderness (Exodus 32:1ff). Though God had been so caring to the people they rebelled in the most ungrateful of ways. God miraculously guided them by the cloud and fire, he gave them his spirit to instruct them (Nehemiah 9:30), he fed them with manna and quail and gave them water to drink out of a desert, he gave them clothes and shoes that did not wear out, he delivered kingdoms into their hands, and brought them to the gateway of Canaan to fulfill his promise he made to Abraham and to their seed. Truly they lacked nothing at all (Nehemiah 9:21). Though God had done so much for them they regarded neither his deity nor mercy.

God is merciful to those who are trying to meet his perfect expectations (see Matthew 5:48; 1 Peter 1:15-16; 2 Peter 1:4 and 1 John 4:17). There are two aspects of God's mercy to consider. First, God's blessing of forgiveness is granted to man yet there is nothing that we have done to deserve this (Romans 4:2 and Ephesians 2:8-9). God will clear man of sin for his name's sake (see Ezekiel 36:22-32). Secondly, it is very apparent that God loves and cares for man (John 3:16). The Lord is merciful to sinful man because he desires that we would all be saved (see 2 Peter 3:9 as compared to the words of Ezra regarding God's mercy at Nehemiah 9:17, 19, 27, 28, and 31) (3n).

"**24** *So the children went in and possessed the land, and you subdued before them the inhabitants of the land, the Canaanites, and gave them into their hands, with their kings, and the peoples of the land, that they might do with them as they would.* **25** *And they took fortified cities, and a fat land, and possessed houses full of all good things, cisterns hewn out, vineyards, and olive yards, and fruit-trees in abundance: so they did eat and were filled, and became fat, and* delighted themselves in your great goodness. **26** *Nevertheless they were **disobedient**, and rebelled against you, and cast your law behind their back, and slew your prophets that testified against them to turn them again unto you, and they wrought great provocations.* **27** *Therefore you delivered them into the hand of their adversaries, who distressed them: and in the time of their trouble, when they cried unto you, you heard them from heaven; and according to your manifold mercies you gave them saviors who saved them out of the hand of their adversaries.* **28** *But after they had rest, they did evil again before you; therefore you left them in the hand of their enemies, so that they had the dominion over them: yet when they returned, and cried unto you, you heard from heaven: and many times did you deliver them according to your **mercies**,* **29** *and testified against them, **that you might bring them again unto your law.** Yet they dealt proudly, and hearkened not unto your commandments, but sinned against your ordinances (which if a man do, he shall live in them), and withdrew the shoulder, and hardened their neck, and would not hear.* **30** *Yet many years did you bear with them, and testified against them by your Spirit through your prophets: yet would they not give ear: therefore you gave them into the hand of the peoples of the lands.* **31** *Nevertheless in your manifold **mercies** you did not make a full end of them, nor forsake them; for **you are a gracious and merciful God**"* **(9:24-31).**

After forty years of wandering in the wilderness for their disobedience the people come again to Canaan and take it with the help of God. The people conquered Canaan and possessed their lands, homes, vineyards, and olive groves that they did not construct or plant. Israel lived off God's blessings and became fat and ungrateful. The Israelites went through cycles of sin, servitude, and sorrow in repentance. God would send a deliverer because he cared for them (book of Judges).

God sent prophets to expose Israel's dark deeds and to motivate them to obey his divine commandments. The people; however, killed many of these prophets (see Nehemiah 9:26; Jeremiah 2:30; Luke 11:47; Acts 7:52 and 1 Thessalonians 2:15). The hardening of Israel's heart came in the form of willfully casting God's laws behind their backs, killing the prophets, unwilling to even listen to God's commands, and ungrateful for the sustenance and land they had. The good characteristics of God were depicted throughout these early years of Israel. Though the people of God rebelled in hardness of heart to his divine commands he remained faithful to his covenant he made with Abraham. God was "*good*" (Nehemiah 9:25), "*merciful*" (Nehemiah 9:27, 28, and 31), "*patient*" (Nehemiah 9:30), and "*gracious*" (Nehemiah 9:31). God brought upon the people "*great distress*" (Nehemiah 9:37) that he "*might bring them again unto your law.*" God's divine way of bringing man back to his law and obedience is to distress them.

Nothing has changed today. Though man has done, and continues, to walk in rebellion to God's divine commandments he remains merciful to save everyone (see John 3:16 and 2 Peter 3:9). The Lord continues to demand man's perfect obedience to his laws and commandments (see Matthew 5:48; 1 Peter 1:15-16; 2 Peter 1:4 and 1 John 4:17). When man sins God is merciful to forgive those who repent (1 John 1:8-10). Though so many good and merciful things are at man's disposal the most part has rebelled and rejected his offer of salvation. The picture set before our eyes, as we read Ezra's prayer, is the issue of human life. Man rebels against God's commandments and God corrects the sinner with distressing chastisement as a father does with a son he loves (see Hebrews 12:3-13; Revelation 15:1-2 and 16:8-11).

"*32 Now therefore, our God, the great, the mighty, and the terrible God, who keeps covenant and lovingkindness, let not all the travail seem little before you, that has come upon us, on our kings, on our princes, and on our priests, and on our prophets, and on our fathers, and on all your people, since the time of the kings of Assyria unto this day. 33 Howbeit **you are just in all that is come upon us**; for you have* *dealt truly, but we have done wickedly; **34** neither have our kings, our princes, our priests, nor our fathers, kept your law, nor hearkened unto your commandments and your testimonies wherewith you did testify against them. **35** For they have not served you in their kingdom, and in your great goodness that you gave them, and in the large and fat land which you gave before them, neither turned they from their wicked works. **36** Behold, we are servants this day, and as for the land that you gave unto our fathers to eat the fruit thereof and the good thereof, behold, we are servants in it. **37** And it yields much increase unto the kings whom you have set over us **because of our sins**: also they have power over our bodies, and over our cattle, at their pleasure, and we are in great distress. **38** And yet for all this we make a sure covenant, and write it; and our princes, our Levites, and our priests, seal unto it"* **(9:32-38).**

The final part of Ezra's humble prayer was an admission to sin and purpose to do better. The priest of God acknowledges the hundreds of years that passed by while the people were in rebellion to God's divine commandments. Though God had been merciful to them and was willing to help them in all their troubles they rejected his help. The people of God have been in servitude to other nations from the days of the Assyrians to the current state of servitude to the Medo-Persian Empire *"because of their sins."* Ezra's prayer is that God would consider all the just punishment they had experienced through the years and to not let it all come to nothing. The priest of God begs for another chance so that the people may show him their resolve to serve faithfully. Ezra, on behalf of the people, enters into a covenant with God that expresses their desire to keep his laws and remain faithful to him.

The chapter before us is interesting in light of understanding how God's grace and mercy works. God continued to wait for his people to acknowledge their wrong doings and follow his laws. His mercy and grace was always there for Israel if only they would do his will. If you followed closely the prayer of Ezra you would note how that God was "*just*" in punishing the people all the years they rebelled (see Nehemiah 9:33). Likewise, God continues to plague the wicked today so that they may be moved to repentance (see Revelation 15:1-2 and 16:8-11). The scriptures are filled with the warnings of God chastising the wicked with affliction and hardships in life so that they may repent (see Proverbs 22:5 and Hebrews 12:3-13 to name just a few). It is only when we acknowledge that our troubles are due to our sinful decisions that we will be moved to repent. When troubles and tribulation come to us in life we must figure out why we are suffering. We ought to all look into our tribulation so that we may "*consider*," with a spirit of wisdom, the reason for our suffering (see Haggai 1:7-11) (17e). It may very well be that we are suffering due to sin in our lives. Then again, it may be that God is testing us (see Genesis 22:1; Job 23:10 and 1 Peter 1:6-7). The important thing is to figure out the why so that we may benefit as God desires. If we are being tested let us rejoice and gain great strength (Romans 5:3). If we are being punished let us repent and turn to the Lord in obedience (Nehemiah 9:29).

Questions over Nehemiah Chapter 9

1. Why were the people of Jerusalem fasting with sackcloth and earth upon them?

2. **True or False:** Ezra acknowledged the creative power of God in his prayer.

3. Who did Ezra say that God found to be a faithful man?

4. How did God show his mercy and care to the Hebrews that were in Egyptian bondage till they entered into Canaan? (9:9-25)

5. What caused Israel to refuse obedience to God after he showed them mighty wonders in Egypt?

6. What would cause the people to return to the laws of God?

7. Was God being just or fair when he punished the Israelites for their rebellion?

8. Notice the multitude of "*mercy*" statements in Nehemiah chapter 9. How does God's mercy, during the days of the early Israelites, relate to his mercy toward us today (see Nehemiah 9:17, 19, 27, 28, 31)?

NEHEMIAH CHAPTER 10

Synopsis

At the completion of the city of Jerusalem's walls, Nehemiah records, "*Now the city was wide and large; but the people were few therein, and the houses were not built*" (Nehemiah 7:4). The sparse populace of Jerusalem is cause for the Lord to move Nehemiah to assemble all Israel to Jerusalem to "*be reckoned by genealogy*" (Nehemiah 7:5). When they are all together in Jerusalem the people make a request that Ezra read the Law of God to them (Nehemiah 8:1ff). Ezra does so for seven straight days (Nehemiah 8:18). They find, during the reading, that they are supposed to be keeping the feast of Tabernacles during this time (Nehemiah 8:13-18). Ezra prays on behalf of the people at the completion of the feast (Nehemiah 9). Ezra reviews a history of God's mercy and the people's hard hearted disobedience. Ezra ends the prayer with a request that God's people sign a covenant with God that they would agree to set their heart on knowing and following God's laws (Nehemiah 9:38).

Chapter 10 illustrates the **resolve** of the people to serve God and keep his commandments. Nehemiah, Zedekiah, the 22 priests, 17 Levites, and 44 chiefs of the people signed a covenant agreement with God that gave an oath of their purpose to "*walk in God's law*" (Nehemiah 10:29). Furthermore they had resolve regarding God's holy temple. The people said, "*and we will not forsake the house of our God*" (Nehemiah 10:39).

Application

God expects all people to walk in perfect obedience to his laws in every generation (Matthew 5:48; Galatians 3:10; 1 Peter 1:15-16; 2 Peter 1:4; 1 John 4:17 to name a few passages). God desires all men to enter into a covenant agreement with him to receive the blessed fruits of obedience or the curses of disobedience (Nehemiah 10:29 and 2 Peter 3:9). When we are baptized into Christ for the forgiveness of sins we are added to the Lord's church (Acts 2:38-44) and belong to Christ (Acts 20:28 and 1 Corinthians 6:19-20). We are now his servants and expected to not sin (Romans 6:1-4, 11). I gain a greater understanding of the world I live in as I look into God's word and his covenants. God governs the world of men (Jeremiah 32:27). The Lord chastises the wicked with plagues or a curse when they sin (Deuteronomy 28:58-62; 29:22-29; Hebrews 12:4-12 and Revelation 15:1-2 and 16:8-11). Those who obey God's laws are blessed and prolong their lives. As long as my approach to life's temptations and questions is "*as it is written in the law*" I will succeed in my Christian life now and forevermore (Nehemiah 10:34-36).

To have resolve is to "make a firm decision about something or to decide by formal vote" (AHD 1052). Nehemiah chapter 10 teaches us that when we have great faith and trust in God we will be more resolved to walk in his commandments. We often sing the song, "I am Resolved" in our song books by J. H. Fillmore. The song is based upon John 6:68 when Peter said, "68 *Lord, to whom shall we go? You have the words of eternal life.*" Peter and the other disciples of Jesus had the opportunity to turn away from the Lord after his sermon of hard sayings; however, they had resolved to follow the Lord because they had seen his miracles and heard his authorized words. The disciples had concluded that there was none other to turn to than Jesus. The Apostle Paul illustrated resolve in his life too (see 2 Corinthians 4:16-18; Philippians 3:12-14 and 2 Timothy 4:6-8) (19w). The people in the days of Nehemiah had witnessed God's miraculous help in reconstructing the wall and they had the word of God before them. They are now resolved to follow God's word as you and I must be!

Nehemiah 10

The People Seal a Covenant with God to Illustrate their Resolve to Follow His Laws (10:1-27)

"**1** *Now those that sealed were: Nehemiah the governor, the son of Hacaliah, and Zedekiah,* **2** *Seraiah, Azariah, Jeremiah,* **3** *Pashhur, Amariah, Malchijah,* **4** *Hattush, Shebaniah, Malluch,* **5** *Harim, Meremoth, Obadiah,* **6** *Daniel, Ginnethon, Baruch,* **7** *Meshullam, Abijah, Mijamin,* **8** *Maaziah, Bilgai, Shemaiah; these were the priests*" **(10:1-8)**.

A list of all those who signed and sealed the covenant agreement with God (detailed at Nehemiah 10:28ff) is now given. The first to sign was Nehemiah the governor. Following Nehemiah's signature was 22 priests.

"**9** *And the Levites: namely, Jeshua the son of Azaniah, Binnui of the sons of Henadad, Kadmiel;* **10** *and their brethren, Shebaniah, Hodiah, Kelita, Pelaiah, Hanan,* **11** *Mica, Rehob, Hashabiah,* **12** *Zaccur, Sherebiah, Shebaniah,* **13** *Hodiah, Bani, Beninu*" **(10:9-13)**.

Seventeen Levites signed the covenant document that illustrated a purpose to serve God in fear and obedience. It may be that these Levites were heads of their families.

"**14** *The chiefs of the people: Parosh, Pahath-moab, Elam, Zattu, Bani,* **15** *Bunni, Azgad, Bebai,* **16** *Adonijah, Bigvai, Adin,* **17** *Ater, Hezekiah, Azzur,* **18** *Hodiah, Hashum, Bezai,* **19** *Hariph, Anathoth, Nobai,* **20** *Magpiash, Meshullam, Hezir,* **21** *Meshezabel, Zadok, Jaddua,* **22** *Pelatiah, Hanan, Anaiah,* **23** *Hoshea, Hananiah, Hasshub,* **24** *Hallohesh, Pilha, Shobek,* **25** *Rehum, Hashabnah, Maaseiah,* **26** *and Ahiah, Hanan, Anan,* **27** *Malluch, Harim, Baanah*" **(10:14-27)**.

The chiefs of the people were the heads of the other non-Levite families. There are a total of 44 chiefs named. These would be significant signatures on the covenant document because of their influence among the people they were over.

The Covenant Agreement (10:28-39)

"**28** *And the rest of the people, the priests, the Levites, the porters, the singers, the Nethinim, and all that had separated themselves from the peoples of the lands unto the law of God, their wives, their sons, and their daughters, every one that had knowledge and understanding;* **29** *they clave to their brethren, their nobles, and entered into a curse, and into an oath,* **to walk in God's law,** *which was given by Moses the servant of God, and to observe and do all the commandments of Jehovah our Lord, and his ordinances and his statutes;*" **(10:28-29).**

The people have listened to Ezra read much out of the Mosaic Law. They have kept the feast of Tabernacles (Nehemiah 8:13-18). They have separated themselves from foreign wives (Ezra 9) and the wicked people of the nations. The people now "*cleave to their brethren*" (Nehemiah 10:29 and 9:1-3). The people show great **resolve** to follow God's laws by entering into the covenant agreement as did the governor and nobles mentioned above.

The seal of their purpose was to enter into a "*curse and oath to walk in God's laws.*" The "*curse*" that the people acknowledge and agree to is that if they rebel against God's commandments he will chastise them so that they repent (see Deuteronomy 28:58-62 and 29:22-29 as compared to Hebrews 12:3-13 and Revelation 16:8-11). All divine laws demand perfect obedience (see Galatians 3:10 and Romans 2:13). God's expectation for his people of every age is perfect obedience (Galatians 3:10; Matthew 5:48; 1 Peter 1:15-16 etc.). Christians make a similar covenant with God today at baptism (see Romans 6:1-11). The life of Abraham is a great example of one who purposed in life to live by God's laws (see Romans 4).

The "*rest of the people*" would be those not listed as priests, Levites, porters, singers, and the Nethinim. The "*porters*" were the gatekeepers (ISBE volume 3, page 909). The "*singers*" were the descendants of Korah's sons that were chosen by David to preside over music in the house of Jehovah (see 1 Chronicles 6:22-23, 31). Heman, a latter descendant of Korah, was known as a "*singer*" (1 Chronicles 6:33). Heman's sons would later serve as prophets of musical instruments whose duty was to sing songs in the house of God and at set feast days (1 Chronicles 25:1, 6; 2 Chronicles 5:12 and 35:15). The sons of Korah and the sons of Asaph and Jeduth were Levites whose official duty was to sing songs of praise to God (see 2 Chronicles 5:12 and Nehemiah 7:44).

The "*Nethinim*" were likely servants in the temple of God (see Ezra 8:20). Josephus referred to the Nethinim as temple slaves (Ant. Xi.5.1 [128]). "One may thus assume that the Nethinim were originally foreign slaves, mostly prisoners of war, who were given to the temple and assigned the lower menial duties there" (ISBE, volume 3, page 525).

"**30** *and that we would not give our daughters unto the peoples of the land, nor take their daughters for our sons;* **31** *and if the peoples of the land bring wares or any grain on the Sabbath day to sell, that we would not buy of them on the Sabbath, or on a holy day; and that we would forego the seventh year, and the exaction of every debt*" **(10:30-31).**

As Ezra read the Law of Moses in the hearing of the people they no doubt ran across Exodus 34:14-17 and Deuteronomy 7:3. These passages command the people of Israel not to marry the Canaanites. Ezra was moved to great sorrow and indignation when he found that the people had done this very thing at Ezra 9-10. Though Israel was not permitted to marry the foreign women or take to friend the wicked they were permitted to do business with them.

The covenant that Israel now enters in with God states that they would no longer marry the foreign women and neither would they do business on the Sabbath day with those of the world. The Sabbath was a holy day that was to be kept sacred (i.e., no work but rather rest and worship) (Exodus 20:8-11). These verses infer that the people of God were authorized to do business with the world at other times of the week. When we read of the command in the New Testament to "*be not equally yoked with unbelievers*" we know that this is not talking about marriages nor every day dealing with them due to Ezra's instructions and the context of 2 Corinthians 6. Paul is warning Christians not to be yoked in the work of wickedness which is exactly what these Jews were now purposing not to do.

A third resolve, on the part of the Jews, was that they would release those who owed debts on the year of "*Jehovah's release*" (see Deuteronomy 15:1-2). The people had not only a "*mind to work*" but a mind to be convicted and obey the truths found in the law of God (see Nehemiah 4:6).

"**32** *Also we made ordinances for us, to charge ourselves yearly with the third part of a shekel for the service of the house of our God;* **33** *for the showbread, and for the continual meal offering, and for the continual burnt-offering, for the Sabbaths, for the new moons, for the set feasts, and for the holy things, and for the sin-offerings to make atonement for Israel, and for all the work of the house of our God*" **(10:32-33).**

The command to pay the yearly half shekel (or one third) is given at Exodus 30:13 (1d). The yearly contribution was for the service and worship at the temple in the form of various sacrifices, offerings, and set feasts. This contribution had obviously not been observed yet the people now resolve to do so.

"**34** *And we cast lots, the priests, the Levites, and the people, for the wood-offering, to bring it into the house of our God, according to our fathers' houses, at times appointed, year by year, to burn upon the* altar of Jehovah our God, **as it is written in the law**; **35** *and to bring the first-fruits of our ground, and the first-fruits of all fruit of all manner of trees, year by year, unto the house of Jehovah;* **36** *also the first-born of our sons, and of our cattle,* **as it is written in the law**, *and the firstlings of our herds and of our flocks, to bring to the house of our God, unto the priests that minister in the house of our God*" **(10:34-36).**

The repeated statements, "*as it is written in the law*" illustrate a reverential respect for the word of God. The mind of the people was to do all things according to God's commandments. Today, we see the same mindset being encouraged by the Lord. The Apostle Paul wrote, "*17 And whatsoever you do in word or deed do all in the name of the Lord Jesus giving thanks to the Father through him*" (Colossians 3:17). Doing all that was written in the "*law*" would give them escape from the divine wrath of God and his curse upon the disobedient.

The people determine to bring wood offerings to burn upon the altar of Jehovah. The Law of Moses called for the wood upon the altar to burn continually (see Leviticus 6:12ff). The people, upon hearing the command to offer the first fruits of their harvest (Deuteronomy 26:1-2), trees (Leviticus (19:23), sons for sanctification (Numbers 18:16) and cattle (Numbers 18:15), did so with joyous hearts.

"**37** *and that we should bring the first-fruits of our dough, and our heave-offerings, and the fruit of all manner of trees, the new wine and the oil, unto the priests, to the chambers of the house of our God; and the tithes of our ground unto the Levites; for they, the Levites, take the tithes in all the cities of our tillage.* **38** *And the priest the son of Aaron shall be with the Levites, when the Levites take tithes: and the Levites shall bring up the tithe of the tithes unto the house of our God, to the chambers, into the treasure-house.* **39** *For the children of Israel and the children of Levi shall bring the heave-offering of the grain, of the new wine, and of the oil, unto the chambers, where are the vessels of the sanctuary, and the priests that minister, and the porters, and the singers: and* **we will not forsake the house of our God**" **(10:37-39).**

Moses laid out commandments to the people of God so that the priests would be financially supported as they performed the work of the temple of God (see Numbers 4:15 and 18:17). The tithe offerings were taken to the chambers of the temple and there stored for the priests. Additionally, the people were to pay a tithe (tenth) of all their goods annually to the priests and these goods were also stored in the chambers of the temple. Today, preachers and elders have this right over God's people (see 1 Corinthians 9:6-14 and 1 Timothy 5:17-18). New Testament Christians do not tithe to accomplish this work but rather they give as they have been prospered (see 1 Corinthians 16:2).

The people, with the voice of resolve, proclaim "*and we will not forsake the house of our God.*" The people had resolved to do better in the future then what they had done in the past. They had obviously forsaken the burnt offering, tithes, set feasts days, the Sabbath day and so forth. Christians today may "forsake the house of God" by not performing the acts of worship that God commands. The Lord commands the assembly (Acts 20:7ff and Hebrews 10:26-28) where giving, singing, preaching, partaking of the Lord's Supper, and praying takes place. Furthermore the "*house of our God*" stands for the Christians who share a like precious faith not only on a local setting but a world wide area. God's command is that we love and help each other along life's way (see James 2:15; 1 Peter 2:17 and 1 John 3:15-17).

Questions over Nehemiah Chapter 10

1. What was the covenant that the people entered into with the Lord?

2. Explain the covenant that New Testament Christians enter into when they obey the gospel?

3. Are New Testament Christians similarly commanded to "*observe and do all the commandments of the Lord our God?*" (see Nehemiah 10:29)

4. What did the statements, "*as it is written in the law*" (Nehemiah 10:34-36) and "*we will not forsake the house of our God*" (Nehemiah 10:39) say about the people's resolve?

NEHEMIAH CHAPTER 11

Synopsis

Nehemiah gives an account of every person who would dwell in Jerusalem by lot or voluntarily. Each class of people represents a specific contribution to the overall welfare of the city. Nehemiah lists not only those in charge of spiritual duties in the temple of God but also those who would guard and protect the city as mighty men of valor. God's people have a new beginning. The city of Jerusalem and surrounding lands of Judah were wide open and sparsely populated. Now was their time to rebuild the kingdom of God and move closer to the day that Jesus would fulfill God's promise to bless all nations through the seed of Abraham.

Application

God fulfills his promises (Jeremiah 30:18-24). The prophet Isaiah was so sure the people would return from Babylonian captivity that he spoke of the event as though it had already happened years before it actually did (Isaiah 11:11-16). Nehemiah sets up specific people to dwell in the cities of Judah and Benjamin so that worship and protection from enemies may be achieved. Likewise, the church has been blessed with all types of people that come together to do their part in the work, worship, and protection of the kingdom of God or church (see 1 Corinthians 12:12ff).

Nehemiah 11

Repopulating Jerusalem (11 all)

"**1** *And the princes of the people dwelt in Jerusalem: the rest of the people also cast lots, to bring one of ten to dwell in Jerusalem the holy city, and nine parts in the other cities.* **2** *And the people blessed all the men that willingly offered themselves to dwell in Jerusalem*" **(11:1-2).**

Apparently Jerusalem was not the most popular place to live. We are not told why this is but it was possibly due to the stigma of war, desolation, and harsh death associated with the city's history. Many may have been afraid to live in the city (see Jeremiah 19:9). We now have a greater understanding of why God moved Nehemiah to gather all the people to the city of Jerusalem to be numbered according to their genealogies (Nehemiah 7:5).

The object of accounting for the people and their genealogies appears to be three fold. First, the people were to providentially hear the word of God read so that corrections would be made to their lives (Nehemiah 9). Secondly, the genealogies were to be correctly registered to see to it that qualified priest were serving in the tabernacle (see Nehemiah 7:64). Lastly, we find that the people were assembled together so that lots may be cast in order to determine who would live in Jerusalem. Some families voluntarily moved to Jerusalem and they were blessed for doing so.

"**3** *Now these are the chiefs of the province that dwelt in Jerusalem: but in the cities of Judah dwelt every one in his possession in their cities, to wit, Israel, the priests, and the Levites, and the Nethinim, and the children of Solomon's servants.* **4** *And in Jerusalem dwelt certain of the children of Judah, and of the children of Benjamin. Of the children of Judah: Athaiah the son of Uzziah, the son of Zechariah, the son of Amariah, the son of Shephatiah, the son of Mahalalel, of the children of Perez;* **5** *and Maaseiah the son of Baruch, the son of Colhozeh, the son of Hazaiah, the son of Adaiah, the son of Joiarib, the* son of Zechariah, the son of the Shilonite. *6 All the sons of **Perez** that dwelt in Jerusalem were four hundred threescore and eight valiant men*" **(11:3-6).**

Nehemiah gives an account of the residents of Jerusalem from the tribes of Judah and Benjamin (It is unknown if these are the families whose lot it was to now dwell in Jerusalem, volunteers, or current residents).

The children of Judah appear to be headed by the household of Perez and numbered 468 in valiant men.

"*7 And these are the sons of Benjamin: Sallu the son of Meshullam, the son of Joed, the son of Pedaiah, the son of Kolaiah, the son of Maaseiah, the son of Ithiel, the son of Jeshaiah. 8 And after him Gabbai, Sallai, nine hundred twenty and eight. 9 And Joel the son of Zichri was their overseer; and Judah the son of Hassenuah was second over the city*" **(11:7-9).**

The children of Benjamin living in Jerusalem numbered 928.

The city manager was Joel and he was assisted by Judah.

"*10 Of the priests: Jedaiah the son of Joiarib, Jachin, 11 Seraiah the son of Hilkiah, the son of Meshullam, the son of Zadok, the son of Meraioth, the son of Ahitub, the ruler of the house of God, 12 and their brethren that did the work of the house, eight hundred twenty and two; and Adaiah the son of Jeroham, the son of Pelaliah, the son of Amzi, the son of Zechariah, the son of Pashhur, the son of Malchijah, 13 and his brethren, chiefs of fathers' houses, two hundred forty and two; and Amashsai the son of Azarel, the son of Ahzai, the son of Meshillemoth, the son of Immer, 14 and their brethren, mighty men of valor, a hundred twenty and eight; and their overseer was Zabdiel, the son of Haggedolim*" **(11:10-14).**

There appears to be a mix of all necessary people to inhabit, protect, and serve God in the city of Jerusalem. The priests in Jerusalem numbered 822. Chiefs of father's houses numbered 242. Amashsai's descendants numbered 128 mighty men of valor.

"**15** *And of the Levites: Shemaiah the son of Hasshub, the son of Azrikam, the son of Hashabiah, the son of Bunni;* **16** *and Shabbethai and Jozabad, of the chiefs of the Levites, who had the oversight of the outward business of the house of God;* **17** *and Mattaniah the son of Mica, the son of Zabdi, the son of Asaph, who was the chief to begin the thanksgiving in prayer, and Bakbukiah, the second among his brethren; and Abda the son of Shammua, the son of Galal, the son of Jeduthun.* **18** *All the Levites in the holy city were two hundred fourscore and four.* **19** *Moreover the porters, Akkub, Talmon, and their brethren, that kept watch at the gates, were a hundred seventy and two*" **(11:15-19).**

Levites dwelling in Jerusalem numbered 284. Many of these people did various services of the temple that were not associated with priestly duties. There were porters dwelling in Jerusalem that were responsible for keeping watch at the gates of the city. Again, every aspect of daily life and the necessities to live in peace were to be met by the specific people and their duties.

"**20** *And the residue of Israel, of the priests, the Levites, were in all the cities of Judah, every one in his inheritance.* **21** *But the Nethinim dwelt in Ophel: and Ziha and Gishpa were over the Nethinim.* **22** *The overseer also of the Levites at Jerusalem was Uzzi the son of Bani, the son of Hashabiah, the son of Mattaniah, the son of Mica, of the sons of Asaph, the singers, over the business of the house of God.* **23** *For there was a commandment from the king concerning them, and a settled provision for the singers, as every day required.* **24** *And Pethahiah the son of Meshezabel, of the children of Zerah the son of Judah, was at the king's hand in all matters concerning the people*" **(11:20-24).**

King Artaxerxes commanded provisions to be given to the "*sons of Asaph, the singers, over the business of the house of God.*" Asaph was a Levite (1 Chronicles 6:39). He was also a prophet, poet (2 Chronicles 29:30 and Nehemiah 12:46) and musician (Nehemiah 12:46). David appointed Asaph, along with Heman and Ethan, to presided over the singing and music during worship (1 Chronicles 15:16-19). Asaph's sons all followed in their father's footsteps as a musician in the worship of God (1 Chronicles 25:1-2 and 2 Chronicles 20:14). Asaph is the author of Psalms such as chapter 50.

Through time, the descendants of Korah's sons were chosen by David to preside over music in the house of Jehovah (see 1 Chronicles 6:22-23, 31). Heman, a latter descendant of Korah, was known as a *"singer"* (1 Chronicles 6:33). Heman's sons would later serve as prophets of musical instruments whose duty was to sing songs in the house of God and at set feast days (1 Chronicles 25:1, 6; 2 Chronicles 5:12 and 35:15). The sons of Korah and the sons of Asaph and Jeduth were Levites whose official duty was to sing songs of praise to God (see 2 Chronicles 5:12 and Nehemiah 7:44 and 11:22).

*"**25** And as for the villages, with their fields, some of the children of Judah dwelt in Kiriath-arba and the towns thereof, and in Dibon and the towns thereof, and in Jekabzeel and the villages thereof, **26** and in Jeshua, and in Moladah, and Beth-pelet, **27** and in Hazar-shual, and in Beer-sheba and the towns thereof, **28** and in Ziklag, and in Meconah and in the towns thereof, **29** and in En-rimmon, and in Zorah, and in Jarmuth, **30** Zanoah, Adullam, and their villages, Lachish and the fields thereof, Azekah and the towns thereof. So they encamped from Beer-sheba unto the valley of Hinnom. **31** The children of Benjamin also dwelt from Geba onward, at Michmash and Aija, and at Beth-el and the towns thereof, **32** at Anathoth, Nob, Ananiah, **33** Hazor, Ramah, Gittaim, **34** Hadid, Zeboim, Neballat, **35** Lod, and Ono, the valley of craftsmen. **36** And of the Levites, certain courses in Judah were joined to Benjamin"* **(11:25-36).**

Nehemiah gives a record of the other places in Judah and Benjamin where the people would dwell. The land was wide open and the people relatively sparse. They had a new beginning and God had fulfilled his promise to return them to the land after seventy years of Babylonian captivity.

Questions over Nehemiah Chapter 11

1. **True or False:** The general population desired to live in Jerusalem.

2. Why do you suppose Nehemiah chose priest, mighty men of valor, singers, gate and wall guards, and a variety of other people to dwell in Jerusalem?

3. What does Nehemiah chapter 11 suggest about God's promise to free his people from Babylonian captivity? (see Isaiah 11:11-16 and Jeremiah 30:18-24)

NEHEMIAH CHAPTER 12

Synopsis

Nehemiah chapter 12 records the dedication of the wall around Jerusalem. The people march in two groups making sacrifices and singing songs of praise to God with musical instruments according to the commandment of David. Nehemiah leads one group and Ezra the other. The people's hearts are filled with joy and resolve to keep all the commandments of God.

Application

Nehemiah chapter 12 teaches us lessons on how to understand the use of the Old Testament. First, we understand that application must be made from these Old Testament books (see 1 Corinthians 10:11 and Romans 15:4). Secondly, we know that whenever Old Testament practices are brought over into the New Testament they are binding on Christians today. Murder was a sin in the Old Testament just as it is a sin today. Sacrifices and special days; however, are totally different from the Old Testament to the New. While sacrifices were made upon the altar of burnt offering in the Old Testament days Christians today are required to only make spiritual sacrifices of righteousness and holiness (Hebrews 13). Furthermore we do not assemble for worship to God on the Sabbath (Exodus 20:8-11) but rather the first day of the week (Acts 20:7 and 1 Corinthians 16:1-2).

When it comes to musical instruments used in the worship services we find them throughout the Old Testament because it was the *"commandment of David the man of God"* (see Nehemiah 12:24-27, 36). The Psalms are filled with specific instructions to sing with instruments of music too. When we move to the New Testament; however, the musical instrument is noticeably absent. The Apostle Paul commands that singing with the voice or heart take place in worship to God (see Ephesians 5:19 and Colossians 3:16). The conclusion is that God no longer desires the instrument to be used in worship because he commands singing with the voice.

Nehemiah 12

The Levites and Priests who dwelled in Jerusalem and its Provinces (12:1-27)

*"**1** Now these are **the priests** and the Levites that went up with Zerubbabel the son of Shealtiel, and Jeshua: Seraiah, Jeremiah, Ezra, **2** Amariah, Malluch, Hattush, **3** Shecaniah, Rehum, Meremoth, **4** Iddo, Ginnethoi, Abijah, **5** Mijamin, Maadiah, Bilgah, **6** Shemaiah, and Joiarib, Jedaiah. **7** Sallu, Amok, Hilkiah, Jedaiah. These were the chiefs of the priests and of their brethren in the days of Jeshua. **8** Moreover **the Levites**: Jeshua, Binnui, Kadmiel, Sherebiah, Judah, [and] Mattaniah, who was over the thanksgiving, he and his brethren. **9** Also Bakbukiah and Unno, their brethren, were over against them according to their offices. **10** And Jeshua begat Joiakim, and Joiakim begat Eliashib, and Eliashib begat Joiada, **11** and Joiada begat Jonathan, and Jonathan begat Jaddua. **12** And in the days of Joiakim were priests, heads of fathers' houses: of Seraiah, Meraiah; of Jeremiah, Hananiah; **13** of Ezra, Meshullam; of Amariah, Jehohanan; **14** of Malluchi, Jonathan; of Shebaniah, Joseph; **15** of Harim, Adna; of Meraioth, Helkai; **16** of Iddo, Zechariah; of Ginnethon, Meshullam; **17** of Abijah, Zichri; of Miniamin, of Moadiah, Piltai; **18** of Bilgah, Shammua; of Shemaiah, Jehonathan; **19** and of Joiarib, Mattenai; of Jedaiah, Uzzi; **20** of Sallai, Kallai; of Amok, Eber; **21** of Hilkiah, Hashabiah; of Jedaiah, Nethanel. **22** As for the Levites, in the days of*

*Eliashib, Joiada, and Johanan, and Jaddua, there were recorded the heads of fathers' houses; also the priests, in the reign of Darius the Persian. 23 The sons of Levi, heads of fathers' houses, were written in the book of the chronicles, even until the days of Johanan the son of Eliashib. 24 And the chiefs of the Levites: Hashabiah, Sherebiah, and Jeshua the son of Kadmiel, with their brethren over against them, to praise and give thanks, **according to the commandment of David the man of God**, watch next to watch. 25 Mattaniah, and Bakbukiah, Obadiah, Meshullam, Talmon, Akkub, were porters keeping the watch at the store-houses of the gates. 26 These were in the days of Joiakim the son of Jeshua, the son of Jozadak, and in the days of Nehemiah the governor, and of Ezra the priest the scribe"* **(12:1-26).**

The above list of names is a compilation of those that had come up from Babylon with Zerubbabel and Jeshua the high priest. Most of these same names were given at Nehemiah 10:1-9 as those who had signed the agreement to keep all of God's commandments. Twenty two heads of the priests are enumerated in verses one through seven and the heads of the Levites are given in verses 8-9, 22-24.

Notice that the gathering of priests, Levites, and singers for the dedication of the wall was in accordance with the "*commandment of David the man of God*." David had commanded dedications to holy things of God such as the Ark of the Covenant when it was brought into Jerusalem after being held by the Philistines (1 Chronicles 16:4) and the cleansing of the temple by Hezekiah (2 Chronicles 29:25). David's influence and divinely inspired guidance of the people continued to be felt and adhered to as divine ordinances. David was not only a king to Israel but a prophet who taught the people God's will (see Acts 2:29-30).

The dedication of the wall of Jerusalem (12:27-47)

"27 And at the dedication of the wall of Jerusalem they sought the Levites out of all their places, to bring them to Jerusalem, to keep the dedication with gladness, both with thanksgivings, and with singing,

114

with cymbals, psalteries, and with harps. **28** *And the sons of the singers gathered themselves together, both out of the plain round about Jerusalem, and from the villages of the Netophathites;* **29** *also from Beth-gilgal, and out of the fields of Geba and Azmaveth: for the singers had built them villages round about Jerusalem.* **30** *And the priests and the Levites purified themselves; and they purified the people, and the gates, and the wall"* **(12:27-30).**

All the Levites were sought out and brought to Jerusalem for the dedication of the wall (a ceremony indicating that the wall of Jerusalem is to be set apart as holy). God had providentially cared for the people as they constructed it. The people show their gratitude and acknowledgment of God's help by performing a spiritual dedication ceremony to the Lord.

According to the *"commandment of David"* the singers were to sing with *"cymbals, psalteries, and with harps."* David had commanded this type of worship when the Ark of the Covenant was brought to Jerusalem and placed in the city of David (1 Chronicles 15:16). David had commanded that a portion of Levites be numbered and assigned to singing praises to God with instruments (see 1 Chronicles 23:1-6) (this is apparently the *"singers"* under consideration here in Nehemiah). David had also commanded that specific prophets were to *"prophesy with harps, with psalteries, and with cymbals:"* (1 Chronicles 25:1ff).

Some today would say that this is their authority for using musical instruments in New Testament worship. Notice; however, that as Israel is back in their home land they are fulfilling the written *"law of Moses"* (see Ezra 3:2). Jesus nailed the Mosaic Law to the cross and it has no authority over Christians other than the commandments, such as murder, that are brought into the New Testament (see Colossians 2:14 and Galatians 5:4). One must take notice that the commandments regarding singing with musical instruments are very clear in the Old Testament. Especially is this so in the Psalms where David often wrote in the superscriptions the actual instrument that he intended the song to be sung with. There is an obvious absence of musical instruments in the New Testament. When the command to sing is given we are simply told to sing with our voice and heart rather than an instrument (see Ephesians 5:19). If God would have wanted us to use instruments of worship in the New Testament church he would have told us. His command; however, was that we sing with the heart (see Colossians 3:16) (12u).

A great lesson is learned throughout a study of God's word in relation to how I am to interpret it. When God gives us commandments that he expects us to follow he does not express endless other options that people could do. For example, the Lord reveals that we are to worship on the first day of the week at Acts 20:7. God does not have to say "thou shalt not partake of the Lord's Supper in worship on Monday, Tuesday, etc." He tells us what we need to know about a subject and we are not at liberty to change his commands. Secondly, we must learn to respect the authorized silence of the scriptures. If God commands that we sing with our hearts we should be satisfied with this and not seek to add things, like instruments, to his divine instructions. We learn this valuable lesson when looking at Hebrews 7:11ff. The author of Hebrews tells us that God ordained the priest to be of the tribe of Levi. God did not have to say that the priest were not to be of the tribes of Gad, Reuben, Benjamin, and so forth.

When one examines God's commands against idolatry at Exodus 20:24-26 and then compares these statements with Deuteronomy 4:15 one gains a better understanding of God's methods of commanding. God said do this and he does not have to say, in relation to that law, don't do this, that, and all else. Let us learn to respect God's authority.

The priests, Levites, all the people, and gates of the wall were purified. Though unsaid, it is likely that sacrifices were made on behalf of the people.

"**31** *Then I brought up the princes of Judah upon the wall, and appointed two great companies that gave thanks and went in procession; whereof one went on the right hand upon the wall toward the dung gate:* **32** *and after them went Hoshaiah, and half of the princes of Judah,* **33** *and Azariah, Ezra, and Meshullam,* **34** *Judah, and Benjamin, and Shemaiah, and Jeremiah,* **35** *and certain of the priests' sons with trumpets: Zechariah the son of Jonathan, the son of Shemaiah, the son of Mattaniah, the son of Micaiah, the son of Zaccur, the son of Asaph;* **36** *and his brethren, Shemaiah, and Azarel, Milalai, Gilalai, Maai, Nethanel, and Judah, Hanani,* **with the musical instruments of David the man of God**; and Ezra the scribe was before them.* **37** *And by the fountain gate, and straight before them, they went up by the stairs of the city of David, at the ascent of the wall, above the house of David, even unto the water gate eastward*" **(12:31-37).**

Nehemiah divided the people into two groups after the gates, wall, and people are purified by sacrifices. The two groups were to march in opposite directions on top of the city wall. Ezra, the priest and scribe, led one group and Nehemiah led the second group. Note once again that the "*musical instruments of David the man of God*" were to accompany them. The phrase, "*of David*" specifically indicates that he is the source of their authority for doing such a thing. David did this and even commanded it (12u).

"**38** *And the other company of them that gave thanks went to meet them, and I after them, with the half of the people, upon the wall, above the tower of the furnaces, even unto the broad wall,* **39** *and above the gate of Ephraim, and by the old gate, and by the fish gate, and the tower of Hananel, and the tower of Hammeah, even unto the sheep gate: and they stood still in the gate of the guard.* **40** *So stood the two companies of them that gave thanks in the house of God, and I, and the half of the rulers with me;* **41** *and the priests, Eliakim, Maaseiah, Miniamin, Micaiah, Elioenai, Zechariah, and Hananiah, with trumpets;* **42** *and Maaseiah, and Shemaiaih, and Eleazar, and*

*Uzzi, and Jehohanan, and Malchijah, and Elam, and Ezer. And the singers sang loud, with Jezrahiah their overseer. **43** And they offered great sacrifices that day, and rejoiced; for God had made them rejoice with great joy; and the women also and the children rejoiced: so that the joy of Jerusalem was heard even afar off'* **(12:38-43).**

As the two groups went along, the singers sang loud and offerings were made to God in a spirit of happiness and joy. The people had gone from extreme sorrow and grief over their sins, to being purified with the gates and walls of the holy city, and now greatly joyous. They were not separated from God! There was hope for eternal life!

Nehemiah led one group and Ezra the other.

"**44** *And on that day were men appointed over the chambers for the treasures, for the heave-offerings, for the first-fruits, and for the tithes, to gather into them, according to the fields of the cities, the portions appointed by the law for the priests and Levites: for Judah rejoiced for the priests and for the Levites that waited. **45** And **they kept the charge of their God**, and the charge of the purification, and so did the singers and the porters, **according to the commandment of David, and of Solomon his son**. **46** For in the days of David and Asaph of old **there was a chief of the singers**, and songs of praise and thanksgiving unto God. **47** And all Israel in the days of Zerubbabel, and in the days of Nehemiah, gave the portions of the singers and the porters, as every day required: and they set apart that which was for the Levites; and the Levites set apart that which was for the sons of Aaron.* Finally, **the people are determined to keep all of God's commands**" **(12:44-47).**

Verse 45 indicates, once again, the people's resolve to keep God's commandments (this included supporting the Levites, priests, and even singers in their work).

Nehemiah continues to press the point that the reason the singing with singers and musical instruments occurred was due to the

118

"commandment of David, and of Solomon his son." During the days of David and Asaph a "chief of singers" (see many references in the superscription of the Psalms) was appointed so that songs of praises with musical instruments would be offered to Jehovah God as a show of *"thanksgiving."*

Questions over Nehemiah Chapter 12

1. What did David command in relationship to dedicating things to God?

2. What determines whether Old Testament practices are to be carried over to New Testament and practiced in our day?

3. Should we use musical instruments in worship today?

4. What two men led two groups of people on top of Jerusalem's wall in the dedication ceremony?

NEHEMIAH CHAPTER 13

Synopsis

The more the people of God opened up the law and read from it the more they found they were in error. Israel found that they were in error for having Tobiah the Ammonite dwell in the great chamber of the temple because he was an Ammonite. Furthermore they had erred in relationship to keeping the Sabbath day holy and had even married foreign women again. Nehemiah, like Paul of the New Testament days, deals with the people's error in a meticulous manner. The man of God identifies each error and deals with them out of not only a spirit of duty and conviction but love too.

Application

The more often we open God's word and study it the more we will be convicted and moved to Godly sorrow over our sins. We ought to all be thankful for preachers and elders today who uphold the truth. We ought to be grateful, rather than offended, when God's servants expose our dark deeds and remind us of our duties to keep the laws of God (see Ezekiel 33:10-16 and 2 Peter 3:1). Every local church needs a Nehemiah or apostle Paul who is convicted and willing to deal with each and every case of sin so that brethren's hope of heaven will be real. When we lose sight of God's laws the church will not look like the church of the New Testament. Too many erring churches exist today for us to be added to their sinful ranks. Let us examine the instructions and pattern of God for his church and follow it. Let us not lose our sanctification. If our local churches and sermons preached are not distinctly different than those of the world then we too cannot be distinguished from the people of Ashdod. Let us remain tightly in line with God's established pattern for the church and its worship. May there always be convicted men, who with a mind of love tell us, "*Why is the house of God forsaken.*"

Nehemiah 13

The Levites are Neglected (13:1-14)

"**1** *On that day they read in the book of Moses in the audience of the people; and therein was **found written**, that an Ammonite and a Moabite should not enter into the assembly of God for ever, **2** because they met not the children of Israel with bread and with water, but hired Balaam against them, to curse them: howbeit our God turned the curse into a blessing. **3** And it came to pass, when they had heard the law, that they separated from Israel all the mixed multitude*" (**13:1-3**).

"*On that day*" is an uncertain date. Nehemiah begins at the "*twentieth year of Artaxerxes*" (Nehemiah 2:1). We read about the people of God celebrating the Feast of Tabernacles on the fifteenth day of the seventh month at chapter 8. Chapter 9 remains in this same time frame. When we come to chapter 13 we read that it is the "*thirty second year of Artaxerxes king of Babylon*" (Nehemiah 13:6). Nehemiah had already returned to Babylon to resume his work as cup bearer to the king.

The people were prompted to request another public reading of the Law of Moses that commanded Israel to keep separate from the Ammonite and Moabite. This is now the fourth time that a public reading of the law is mentioned. Ezra had read the law of God for about six straight hours at Nehemiah 8:1-8. The Law is read for seven straight days during the Feast of Tabernacles (Nehemiah 8:17-18). Again, the law is read for about six hours as the people mourn their sins and make confession at Nehemiah 9:1-4. Once again (chapter 13) the law is read in the public. Israel remains resolved to keep all God's laws. A fascinating point to notice is the consequences of opening up the book of God and reading it. When the people opened the book and read it at chapter eight we saw them weeping in grief over their exposed sins. Latter in the chapter we find the people reading and discovering that they had not been keeping the Feast of Tabernacles as they ought to have been doing. Once again the people "*found*" that their relationship with the Ammonites and Moabites was against God's laws. We may all be amazed and more perfectly guided through this life if only we will open our Bibles and read them (19a).

As the law of God is read it is found that "*an Ammonite and a Moabite should not enter into the assembly of God for ever.*" The people of God had "*mixed*" themselves with Ammonite and Moabite people against the will of God. The Moabites and Ammonites were Israel's kinsmen (see Genesis 19:37ff). They should have had pleasure and empathy for Israel; however, they treated them as enemies. As Israel made their exodus from Egypt to Canaan they found their brother nations Ammon and Moab allied and against them. After Israel had defeated Sihon king of the Amorites, they went to battle against Og the king of Bashan. Both kingdoms were routed and their land disposed by the Israelites according to God's commandments (see Numbers 21:21-35). Balak, king of Moab, heard of these battles and had great fear of Israel. He hires a well known prophet by the name of Balaam to curse the people of God so that he might defeat them (Numbers 22:1-6). Each time Balaam tried to curse Israel; however, he blessed them.

Through time the people had forgotten about Balaam's wicked works. The people forgot about the ill treatment of the Ammonites and Moabites. Their lack of familiarity with God's word caused them to be ignorant of God's curse upon these nations. The Lord excluded Ammon and Moab from the congregation of Israel due to their wickedness "*even to the tenth generation*" (see Deuteronomy 23:3-5) or *"for ever"* (Nehemiah 13:1). The New Testament mentions the character of Balaam a few times to illustrate the danger that he and his spirit poses even to the church today (see 2 Peter 2:15; Jude 1:11 and Revelation 2:14).

*"**4** Now before this, Eliashib the priest, who was appointed over the chambers of the house of our God, being **allied unto Tobiah**, **5** had prepared for him a great chamber, where aforetime they laid the meal-offerings, the frankincense, and the vessels, and the tithes of the grain, the new wine, and the oil, which were given by commandment to Levites, and the singers, and the porters; and the heave-offerings for the priests. **6** But in all this time I was not at Jerusalem; for in the two and thirtieth year of Artaxerxes king of Babylon I went unto the king: and after certain days asked I leave of the king, **7** and I came to Jerusalem, and understood the evil that Eliashib had done for Tobiah, in preparing him a chamber in the courts of the house of God"* **(13:4-7).**

Before the law was read to the people, regarding the illegal communion with the Ammonites and Moabites, Eliashib had given Tobiah the Ammonite *"a great chamber"* in the temple of God. Tobiah was the man who laughed God's people to scorn for attempting to rebuild the walls of Jerusalem (Nehemiah 2:19). He had teamed up with Sanballat in an attempt to cause the work of the wall to stop (Nehemiah 4:7-8). Tobiah was also an Ammonite (Nehemiah 4:3). Eliashib is said to be *"allied to Tobiah"* the Ammonite. The reading of the scriptures exposed the sinfulness of Eliashib's relationship with Tobiah and the exceedingly great sin of giving this Ammonite a room in the chambers of the house of God. The great chamber that Eliashib gave Tobiah was the chamber which held all the offerings that the congregation was to give to the priest (one tenth of their sustenance - see Deuteronomy 18:3). The priests were to receive a tenth of the tenth and it was known as the *"heave-offering."*

When the people heard the law regarding the place of the Ammonites and Moabites they knew that Tobiah's place in the temple was a great error. Nehemiah had been away in Babylon when this had happened (back to his duties as the cupbearer to king Artaxerxes). Nehemiah asks leave of the king to return to Jerusalem to see how God's people faired only to find that they had transgressed God's laws. It may very well be that a scout returned to Babylon to report Eliashib's unlawful work of giving Tobiah a room in the temple.

"8 And it grieved me sore: therefore I cast forth all the household stuff of Tobiah out of the chamber. 9 Then I commanded, and they cleansed the chambers: and thither brought I again the vessels of the house of God, with the meal-offerings and the frankincense" **(13:8-9).**

Nehemiah finds Tobiah dwelling in the chamber of the house of God upon arrival in Jerusalem. Nehemiah is filled with grief. Tobiah is cast out of the temple along with all his belongings. Nehemiah then commands that the chambers be cleansed from this defiled guest.

"10 And I perceived that the portions of the Levites had not been given them; so that the Levites and the singers, that did the work, were fled every one to his field. 11 Then **contended I with the rulers,** *and said,* **Why is the house of God forsaken?** *And I gathered them together, and set them in their place"* **(13:10-11).**

It appears that the Levites and singers had been fearfully removed from the temple of God and their place given to Tobiah the Ammonite. They were no longer given the tithes and it may very well be that Tobiah was receiving the holy tithes that belonged to the people of God. If the Levites were not doing the work of the temple of God then worship was halted. The daily, monthly, and annual sacrifices came to an end with Tobiah's presence in the temple.

Nehemiah shames the rulers by contending with them saying, "*Why is the house of God forsaken*?" The rulers and people had previously vowed to "*not forsake the house of our God*" (Nehemiah 10:39b), however, after a little time passes they turned their backs on God's commandments. Tobiah was the source of all their issues. Remember that Tobiah is the son in law of Shecaniah the son of Arah and many people in Jerusalem were sworn to him (see Nehemiah 6:17-19). These times of history illustrate the significance of having a godly man and or men within a congregation of God's people. Wicked brethren bent on having things different than God's revealed plan must always be kept in check. Too many men are weak in the area of confrontation and let wickedness slide. The meek and convicted men of truth; however, will not stand for unauthorized practices. Nehemiah was that meek and convicted man who would not permit the people and Tobiah to change God's revealed pattern of laws and worship.

It seems that the hardest person to apply the truths of God's laws to is our own selves and our family members. We have no problem identifying, marking, and withdrawing from erring members of the body of Christ and false teachers who are not related to us. Yet when it comes to marking a false teacher who is a part of our immediate family we shrink back in preference for the flesh and blood member of our family over Christ. It is one's hatred for Jesus, the truth, and a rebellious spirit toward God's laws that places his family over God's laws. Jesus said, "37 *He that loves his father or mother more than me is not worthy of me; and he that loves his son or daughter more than me is not worthy of me*" (Matthew 10:37). The people permitted their relationship with Tobiah to overrule God's laws and this was not good.

"**12** *Then brought all Judah the tithe of the grain and the new wine and the oil unto the treasuries.* **13** *And I made treasures over the treasuries, Shelemiah the priest, and Zadok the scribe, and of the Levites, Pedaiah: and next to them was Hanan the son of Zaccur, the son of Mattaniah;* **for they were counted faithful,** *and their business was to distribute unto their brethren.* **14** *Remember me, O my God,*

125

*concerning this, and wipe not out **my good deeds that I have done for the house of my God,** and for the observance thereof"* **(13:10-14).**

Nehemiah had previously put his brother Hananiah in charge over Jerusalem because he was *"a faithful man"* (see Nehemiah 7:2). When the Levites blessed the name of God at chapter 9 they mentioned Abraham as one who received the promises of God because he was *"faithful"* (Nehemiah 9:7-8). Once again we find Nehemiah mentioning one's qualification for Godly service being **faithfulness.** Those who are faithful are those who are reverent and respectful toward God's authorized words. The Apostle Paul tells us that the qualification of one who would be a steward of the gospel of Jesus Christ must also be *"faithful"* (1 Corinthians 4:1-2). All that share in the faithfulness of Abraham will be blessed with forgiveness and eternal life (Galatians 3:9). Every church needs faithful men who will fearfully keep God's laws and stand opposed to the rebellious.

Nehemiah quickly corrects the problem of unfaithfulness on the part of the people and asks that God would remember his *"good deeds."* Nehemiah will make this same statement four times in this chapter (see Nehemiah 13:14, 22, 29, and 31). Nehemiah also made this same statement at chapter 5:19. Why would Nehemiah want God to *"remember his good deeds?"* The answer is obvious. God had established his high expectation of man's absolute moral perfection from the days of Adam through Moses and on to the days of Nehemiah (see Romans 5:14). Righteousness could not be attained by keeping the divine laws from the days of Adam to Moses and from Moses to Christ (i.e., the law Adam was under and the Law of Moses) because these laws offered no forgiveness to the transgressor. Abraham *"found"* that he could only be justified by his obedient faith in God's promises to bring a savior into the world (see Romans 4:1-3). Abraham manifests his faith in God's promises through his obedient works (see Genesis 26:4-5; John 3:39; Hebrews 11:17-18 and James 2:21-22). Nehemiah obviously understood how God justified Abraham and sought the same justification (see Genesis 15:6). The scriptures tell us that not only did Abraham and Nehemiah understand God's will in this matter but also others such as Phinehas (Psalms 106:30-31).

Nehemiah finds Israel Profaning the Sabbath (13:15-22)

"**15** *In those days saw I in Judah some men treading winepresses on the Sabbath, and bringing in sheaves, and lading asses therewith; as also wine, grapes, and figs, and all manner of burdens, which they brought into Jerusalem on the Sabbath day: and I testified against them in the day wherein they sold victuals.* **16** *There dwelt men of Tyre also therein, who brought in fish, and all manner of wares, and sold on the Sabbath unto the children of Judah, and in Jerusalem.* **17** *Then I contended with the nobles of Judah, and said unto them, What evil thing is this that you do, and profane the Sabbath day?* **18** *Did not your fathers do this, and did not our God bring all this evil upon us, and upon this city? Yet you bring more wrath upon Israel by profaning the Sabbath*" **(13:15-18).**

At verse eleven Nehemiah contends with the "*rulers*" regarding forsaking the house of God. Now, Nehemiah contends with the "*nobles*" (verse 17) because the Sabbath day has been "*profaned.*" The rulers and nobles were the leaders of the people and responsible for all the people's spiritual well being. The city of Jerusalem did not have the appearance of a city that served Jehovah and his laws even on the Sabbath day. The Sabbath day was to be a day of rest. Absolutely no labor was to take place on this day (Exodus 20:8-11). Nehemiah observed Jerusalem on the Sabbath and found that it looked no different than any other day of the week in that people were working and trading. Nehemiah "*contends*" with the nobles and rulers because they held responsibility over the people's deeds. Nehemiah asks, "*What evil thing is this that you do, and profane the Sabbath day?*"

Nehemiah reminds the nobles and rulers that Israel and Judah had suffered greatly at the hands of Babylon for this same error (see

Jeremiah 17).   The prophet Ezekiel similarly exposed the wickedness of the shepherds of his day saying, "4 *The diseased have you not strengthened, neither have you healed that which was sick, neither have you bound up that which was broken, neither have you brought back that which was driven away, neither have you sought that which was lost; but with force and with rigor have you ruled over them*" (Ezekiel 34:4).   The actions of the nobles, rulers, and people were sure to bring the wrath of God upon the city.

"**19** *And it came to pass that, when the gates of Jerusalem began to be dark before the Sabbath, I commanded that the doors should be shut, and commanded that they should not be opened till after the Sabbath: and some of my servants set I over the gates, that there should no burden be brought in on the Sabbath day*" **(13:19).**

Nehemiah was a man of actions when it came to God's laws being violated.   He takes matters into his own hand and commands that the gates (where trade and commerce took place) be closed the night before the Sabbath and not opened until after the Sabbath.

Nehemiah was so adamant about the keeping of the Sabbath that he set guards over the gate so that no one would enter with goods to trade.

"**20** *So the merchants and sellers of all kind of wares lodged without Jerusalem once or twice.   **21** Then I testified against them, and said unto them, Why do you lodge about the wall? If you do so again, I will lay hands on you.   From that time forth came they no more on the Sabbath*" **(13:20-21).**

Nehemiah had a zero tolerance policy when it came to men violating God's laws.   When the merchants came to Jerusalem and found the gates closed they decided to camp out until the Sabbath was over.   Nehemiah took offense to this in that it was clear that the merchants cared nothing for the Laws of God.   The presence of the merchants would be a temptation to the people of Israel to violate God's Sabbath laws so he removes them completely.

"**22** *And I commanded the Levites that they should purify themselves, and that they should come and keep the gates, to sanctify the Sabbath day. Remember unto me, O my God, this also, and spare me according to the greatness of your lovingkindness*" **(13:22).**

The Levites were just as guilty as the others who violated the Sabbath. Nehemiah commands that they purify themselves and get back to keeping God's laws regarding the Sabbath. God's people often need spiritually minded convicted men to continue an onslaught of Bible teaching and correction for the sake of their souls. Today, the church of Christ needs strong and convicted elders and preachers to keep the people of God motivated to do those things that are surely commanded in God's word to do. Note that Nehemiah identified the problems, warned the guilty involved, and took action to solve the problem. Too many today simply gripe about problems rather than try to solve them. Local churches with great problems are those who are filled with complainers rather than problem solvers. Nehemiah was a problem solver. He saw the problem and did not sweep it under the rug but rather exposed the issues and demanded immediate correction.

A Third Evil Act Detected and Dealt with Sharply (13:23-31)

"**23** *In those days also saw I the Jews that had married women of Ashdod, of Ammon, and of Moab:* **24** *and their children spoke half in the speech of Ashdod, and could not speak in the Jews' language, but according to the language of each people*" **(13:23-24).**

Nehemiah found that God's people had once again polluted themselves with foreign wives (Ezra 10:10-12). The children of these marriages could not even speak the Hebrew tongue. Their language was that of Ashdod (Philistia), the Ammonites, and Moabites. This was an indication that they were far removed from God, his laws, and his people. Israel had lost her distinction from the other nations (19h).

"**25** *And I contended with them, and cursed them, and smote certain of them, and plucked off their hair, and made them swear by God, saying, You shall not give your daughters unto their sons, nor take their daughters for your sons, or for yourselves.* **26 Did not Solomon king of Israel sin by these things**? *Yet among many nations was there no king like him, and he was beloved of his God, and God made him king over all Israel: nevertheless even him did foreign women cause to sin.* **27** *Shall we then hearken unto you to do all this great evil, to trespass against our God in marrying foreign women?*" **(13:25-27).**

The reality of intense contention between Nehemiah and the wicked of Jerusalem comes to life in these verses. The arguments and disagreements between Nehemiah and the sinners was not casual. The matter before the people was a "*great evil*" because it affronted God's laws on marriage (see Exodus 34:14-17 and Deuteronomy 7:3). Though the Law of Moses specifically forbids intermarriage with the Canaanites it is apparent that others (such as the Ashdodites, Ammonites, and Moabites) were included as those who had the potential of causing God's people to sin. Nehemiah uses the example of Solomon in that he married many foreign women and they caused him to worship other gods. If a man like Solomon, king of Israel and beloved of God, can be caused to sin by foreign wives what makes the people of Nehemiah's day think they will have a different outcome? Additionally, the Law of Moses forbade such marriages so the people were in sin.

Remember that Ezra had earlier sat down with the heads of the father's houses to examine each marital case (Ezra 10:16-17). These meetings identified the lawful and unlawful marriages among them and settled the matter. Secondly they further investigated whether or not true conversion of some of the foreign wives, who were married to their men, had honestly occurred. If so, these marriages were not annulled. Consider these marriages that were actually in the lineage of Christ. Ruth the Moabite married Boaz. Rehab, who was not only a harlot but a Canaanite, married Salmon. Uriah the Hittite married a Jewish girl named Bathsheba who latter became David's wife. All of the named marriages happened before the events of Ezra so it is most probable that the issue of conversion had to be examined. If this is the case there was likely a massive amount of people converted to Judaism to avoid breaking up the family. The New Testament has no such laws. We find Christians married to non-Christians with no instructions to get out of those relationships (see 1 Corinthians 7:13 and 1 Peter 3:1). The lesson learned today is perhaps we should earnestly consider who we are marrying and what type of influence they will have on us. Though it is not a sin to marry an unbeliever it is not the wisest thing to do (consider 1 Corinthians 11:16).

Nehemiah's love for God's laws is illustrated in 6 ways in relation to the people marrying foreign women:

a. Nehemiah contended with them over the matter.

b. Nehemiah cursed them for their wicked works.

c. Nehemiah plucked out the hair of some of them.

d. Nehemiah even executed some.

e. He makes the survivors swear by God that they will no longer violate the Lord's marriage laws by marrying foreigners.

f. Lastly, Nehemiah gives the survivors an example (i.e., Solomon) regarding what can happen when one so sins against God.

"**28** *And one of the sons of Joiada, the son of Eliashib the high priest, was son-in-law to Sanballat the Horonite: therefore I chased him from me.* **29** *Remember them, O my God, because they have defiled the priesthood, and the covenant of the priesthood, and the Levites*" **(13:28-29).**

Sanballat mentioned earlier in our study as being allied with Tobiah. Sanballat was grieved and angered when the Jews began building the wall around Jerusalem (Nehemiah 2:10 and 4:1, 7). He also mocked and laughed at Nehemiah and the working Jews as they did the work on the wall of Jerusalem (Nehemiah 2:19 and 4:1). Sanballat went so far as to attempt an assassination on Nehemiah at chapter 6:1-2. Aside from being antagonistic to Nehemiah and the Jews as they sought to obey the commandments of God he was a Horonite. The International Standard Bible Encyclopedia tells us that the Horonites were "probably inhabitants of Beth-horon" (ISBE volume 2 page 758). Beth-horon was located within the region of Canaan or Palestine proper. Sanballat's error is not necessarily where he is from but what he has done. Furthermore, the real issue at hand is the liberal mind of Eliashib the high priest. Eliashib ought to have rooted Tobiah out of the temple and never permitted his family relationship with Sanballat to affect his duty to obey God's commands and uphold the office of High Priest with great honor. Eliashib, though a high priest, permitted his relationship with Tobiah and Sanballat to corrupt his sense of right and wrong.

Nehemiah runs off Sanballat's son-in-law Joiada because Eliashib would not do it. Though the high priest held a degree of great authority in religious matters Nehemiah had to take matters into his own hand. Joiada, a Levite priest, had no right to be married to a Horonite (see Leviticus 21:1-15). This is further proof of the necessity of keeping proper genealogies as we noted earlier in our study.

Nehemiah asks the Lord to remember the wicked works of the people in that they defiled the priesthood. Nehemiah also asked God to remember his good works on four different occasions in this chapter. Like David of old Nehemiah prays that God would be just in his dealings with all men. God promised to bless the obedient and curse the disobedient (Deuteronomy 28:58-62 and 29:22-29).

"**30** *Thus cleansed I them from all foreigners, and appointed charges for the priests and for the Levites, every one in his work;* **31** *and for the* *wood-offering, at times appointed, and for the first-fruits. Remember me, O my God, for good"* **(13:30-31).**

Nehemiah was successful in cleansing the guilty parties of their wrongful marriages. To further see to it that God's ordinances, regarding the burnt-offerings and thank offerings, be kept Nehemiah appoints people in charge of those things to see to it that they are done. Notice all the times that Nehemiah appoints men to oversee the people's compliance of God's laws. Nehemiah appointed his brother Hananiah to be in charge over Jerusalem after he left because he was a faithful man (Nehemiah 7:1-2). Nehemiah appointed men over the heave offerings to see to it that the Levites, singers, and priest were compensated for their work rather than being forced out into the fields to work (Nehemiah 12:44). Nehemiah appointed servants to stand guard at the gates of Jerusalem so that no merchant would camp out waiting for the Sabbath to pass so that they may sell their merchandise (Nehemiah 13:19-20). Furthermore Nehemiah took it upon his own self to cleanse the people and the temple of God from Tobiah and Sanballat's defilement and influence (see Nehemiah 13:7-8, 30-31).

The people of God have a tendency to slide into apostasy in every generation (see the Corinthians and Galatians of the New Testament). The Lord has ordained that elders would superintend the flock of God among them to keep them sound in the faith (1 Peter 5:1-3). Moreover, God has ordained evangelist to reprove, rebuke, and exhort the brethren with all longsuffering and teaching (2 Timothy 4:1-3). Brethren are to be taught to *"remember"* the words of God and it is the duty of the *"remembrancers"* (elders, preachers, and teachers) to do this duty (Isaiah 62:6 and 2 Peter 3:1-2) (18c).

One may ask, "Where was Ezra during these events?" The fact of the matter is that we are not told. He could have died or traveled to another land. Worse yet he may have tolerated the wicked deeds that transpired at the end of Nehemiah. Previous studies of Ezra's love for God's laws seem to militate against the conclusion that he tolerated their wicked works.

Questions over Nehemiah Chapter 13

1. What did the people discover written in the "*book of Moses*" at chapter 13:1-2?

2. What evil thing did Eliashib, the high priest, do for Tobiah while Nehemiah was away?

3. What does Nehemiah do about Tobiah when he returns to Jerusalem?

4. What does Nehemiah say to the rulers of Jerusalem to shame them?

5. What did the people do to profane the Sabbath Day?

6. What did Nehemiah think about the merchants camping out as they waited for the Sabbath to pass?

7. What "*great evil*" had the people committed against God?

8. Who is responsible for keeping the church today clean from sin?

Bible Topics Index

m. Wrath and Anger

n. Mercy

o. Omnipresence

p. Godhead

q. Identity

r. Work

s. Trustworthy

t. Jealous

u. Indwelling of Godhead

v. God of all Flesh

w. Glory

x. Just in Condemning the Wicked

y. Patient and Longsuffering

z. Creator

aa. Not a respecter of Persons

bb. A Rock of Refuge

4. **God the Father**

a. Identity

b. Father Figure to Man

5. **Jesus, The Son of God**

a. Identity

b. Prophecy

c. Deity

d. Work

e. Second Coming

f. Indwelling

g. Resurrection

h. Authority

i. Our Example

j. He Never Quit

k. Preeminence

l. He Alone Saves

m. Ascension into Heaven

n. The Cross

o. The Fullness of Christ

p. Humanity

q. The Perfect Sacrifice

6. **Holy Spirit**

a. Indwelling

b. Gift

a. Direct Statements

b. Apostolic Examples / Example

c. Necessary Inference

d. Expediency

e. The "Law of Equivalence"

f. My Attitude Toward

g. The Example of Christ

h. Things done, "In the Name"

i. Expansion of Teaching

j. Silence

k. The Pattern

10. **Truth**

a. Identity - Law / Covenants / Law of Moses / Law of Christ / Gospel of Jesus Christ

b. Standard (Righteousness and Justice)

c. Distinct

d. Inspiration / Complete

e. Nature - Power / eternal

f. Designed for All

g. We Can and Must Know Truth Alike

h. Things we Cannot Know

i. Reaction to / response

j. Making a distinction between the Faith and Liberty

k. No Man Above the Laws of God

l. Revelation

m. Calling of God

n. Old Testament Laws binding in the New Testament

o. Not Determined by Popular Preacher

p. No Man may Change

q. Type and Antitype

r. Not Defined by Personal Conscience, Opinion, or Conviction

s. General Truths

t. Value of Old Testament

u. Everlasting Covenant

v. No Grey Areas

w. Transforms Lives

x. Simplicity of

11. **Faith**

a. Bible Belief

b. Trust

c. Confidence

d. Obedience

e. Works

f. Delusions

g. Evidences of our Faith

h. Preconceived Religious Faith

12. **The Church**

a. Identity

b. Name

c. Organization

d. Work

e. Worship

f. Autonomy

g. Problems

h. Prophecy

i. Establishment

j. Role of Women

k. Benevolence

l. God's Expectation

m. Nature of

n. God's Love For

o. Discipline

p. Local and Universal

q. Worship

r. Associated with Truth

s. Associated with Life

t. Letter of Commendation

u. Music

v. Determining the Soundness of a Church

w. Elders / Bishops

x. Growth

y. Eternal

z. Deacons

aa. building

bb. Indestructible

cc. Exclusive

13. **Grace**

a. Identity

b. Relationship to Works or Obedience

14. **Sin**

   a. Identity

   b. Nature

   c. Sin Separates Man from God

   d. Why People Choose to Sin

   e. My Attitude Toward Sin

   f. Hard Hearts

   g. Affects of Sin

   h. Shame

   i. Bondage of Sin

   j. Sins of Ignorance

   k. Situational Ethics

   l. Apostasy

   m. Guilt Associated with Sin

   n. Consequences of Sin

   o. Stumbling Blocks

   p. Spiritual Adultery

   q. Sinful Thoughts

   r. Sincerity

   s. Blasphemy

t. When the Wicked are more Righteous than God's People

15. **How Does One Become a Christian?**

   a. Christian's Identity

   b. Redemption

   c. Justification

   d. Reconciliation

   e. Steps of Salvation (hear, believe, repent, confess, be baptized, remain faithful)

   f. Transformation of the Mind from fleshly to spiritual

   g. Few find Justification

   h. Calling on the Name of God

   i. God's Promise to Justify the Faithful

   j. Conditioned upon obedience

   k. Baptism Special Study

   l. Free Will

16. **The Christian's Never Quit Attitude**

   a. Quitting is not an Option

   b. Pressing Forward in Life

   c. Developing and Maintaining Conviction and Faith

   d. Purpose Driven Christian

a. Grow Spiritually / Study

b. Militant in Truth

c. Watchmen

d. Contend / debate for the Faith

e. Influence / Glorify the name of God

f. Government

g. Christian Armor

h. Sanctification / Distinct

i. Know Your Place before Jehovah

j. Relationship to those in the World

k. Caring for the Poor

l. Maintain your Salvation

m. Put all Doctrines to the Test

n. Personal Evangelism

o. Restore the Erring

p. Give God Glory

q. Repentance

r. Fight the good fight of Faith

s. Conformed to the Image of Christ

t. Fasting

u. Longsuffering and patient

v. Sing songs of Praise

w. Resolve to be Holy

20. **Christian Characteristics**

a. Spirit or Character of Man

b. Meek

c. Humble

d. Selfless

e. Integrity

f. Love Others

g. Self Control

h. Christian Virtues

i. Righteous Indignation

j. Making proper Judgments

k. Walk of Life

l. Work Ethic

m. Nature or Natural order of Things

n. Spiritually Minded

o. Spiritual Strength

p. Persecuted

e. Drugs and Alcohol

f. Prejudice

g. Gossip

h. Dangers Associated with Riches

i. Pride

j. Immodest Dress

k. Revenge

l. Rebellion

m. Hypocrisy

n. Respecter of Persons

o. Envy

p. Ungrateful

q. Anger

r. Flattery

s. mind of

t. Putting God to the Test

u. Bragging

26. **Bible Perfection**

a. God's Great Expectation for his Saints

27. **Forgiveness**

a. Pray for

b. No Sin to Hard for God to Forgive

c. Unforgivable Sin

d. Forgive Others

e. Attaining Forgiveness

28. **Miracles**

a. Spiritual Gifts

b. Purpose of Miracles

c. Are People still Performing Miracles?

d. Signs to instill Faith

29. **Various Erroneous Doctrines**

a. The Spirit of Error

b. Judaism

c. Calvinism

d. Institutionalism

e. Premillinnialism

f. Humanism

g. Denominationalism

h. One Cup No Bible Class

i. Marriage, Divorce, and Remarriage

j. Predestination

k. 70 A.D.

l. Once Saved Always Saved

m. Unacceptable Worship

30. **Bible Characters**

a. Noah

b. Abraham

c. Enoch

d. Jacob

e. Job

f. Moses

g. Joseph

h. Samuel

i. Saul

j. David

k. Solomon

l. Jeroboam

m. Ahab

n. Joab

o. Elijah

p. Elisha

q. Joshua

r. Caleb

s. Jehoshaphat

t. Jehu

u. Hezekiah

v. Ahaz

w. Zedekiah

x. Nehemiah

y. Zerubbabel

z. Ezra

aa. Daniel

bb. Nebuchadnezzar

cc. Jesus

dd. The Apostle Paul

ee. Peter

ff. Judas

gg. John the Baptizer

hh. King Herod

ii. Pharisees

37.   **Resurrection**

38.   **Spiritual Delusion**

39.   **A Worthy Woman**

40.   **A Worthy Man**

41.   **The Apostles**

42.   **Bible Doxologies**

43.   **Dating**

44.   **Drugs and Alcohol**

45.   **Wisdom**

46.   **Bible Heart**

47.   **Conscience**

48.   **Lasting Impressions**

49.   **Nations of the World in History**

    a. Assyria

    b. Babylon

    c. Egypt

    d. Roman Empire

    e. Edom

    f. Medo Persian Empire

    g. Grecian Empire

58.   **Day of Judgment**

   a.   End of Time

   b.   No one Escapes

   c.   No Acceptable Excuses for not Obeying the Lord

   d.   No Money, Fame, Nation, Person, or amount of Power will Save the Wicked

   e.   Outcome based on my Works or Actions

59.   **Eternity**

   a.   Time frame

   b.   What Happens after we Die

60.   **Victory**

61.   **Miscellaneous Bible Topics**

   a.   The Death Penalty

   b.   Does God hear the Prayers of Sinners?

   c.   Celebrating Christmas, Easter, and other Holidays

BIBLIOGRAPHY

Dictionaries and Encyclopedias Consulted

Berube, M. S. Second College Edition of the American Heritage Dictionary. Houghton Mifflin Company: Boston, MA 1991.

Bromiley, G. W. The International Standard Bible Encyclopedia (Four Volumes). William B. Eerdmans Publishing Company: Grand Rapids, Michigan 1979.

Bible Consulted and used as main text of study (blue letters):

1901 American Standard Version Bible. Old and New Testaments Translated out of the original tongues. Being the version set forth A. D. 1611 compared with the most ancient authorities and revised A. D. 1881 – 1885. Newly Edited by the American Revision Committee A. D. 1901. Star Bible Publications, Inc. Fort Worth, Texas 1929.

Made in the USA
Middletown, DE
25 July 2022